ANTONIS VASSILAKIS

# KNOSSOS

MYTHOLOGY-HISTORY
GUIDE TO THE ARCHAEOLOGICAL SITE

ΕΚΔΟΣΕΙΣ ADAM EDITIONS


TEL. 6778440-1, 6774662, FAX. 6774663

www.adam.gr
e-mail: adam.editions@adam.gr

# KNOSSOS

TEXT

ANTONIS VASSILAKIS

**ARCHAEOLOGIST**

*Ph.D. University of Crete*

# CONTENTS



Cretan

AKROTIRI
Falasarna
CHANIA
Aptera
RETHYMNO
Samaria
Gorge
Idaean Cave
Chora Sphakion
Palaiochora
Aghia Triada
Kommos

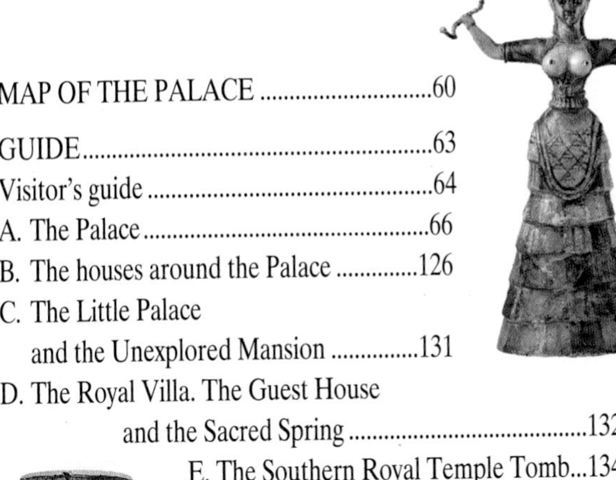

*Sea*

HERAKLEION
Amnisos
KNOSSOS
Malia
Archanes
Diktaean Cave
AGHIOS
NIKOLAOS
Siteia
Palaiokastro
Lato
Zakros
Gournia
Vasiliki
Praissos
Ierapetra

# INTRODUCTION

*The low hill, on which the Neolithic settlement of Knossos developed and where the great palace was later built, was called "Tjelebis Kefala" from the name of the Turkish landowner who sold the area to Sir Arthur Evans. During Minoan times, the hill was the nucleus of the town which also extended over the surrounding hills. In post-Minoan times, the hill with the ruins of the palace was part of the city-state of Knossos, and probably remained un-built, perhaps serving as a place of worship (sacred wood) dedicated to the Mother Goddess.*

# THE NATURAL ENVIRONMENT

The "Kefala" of Knossos is situated in the hilly inland area south of the valleys of Herakleion and Karteros.

Through it runs the Kairatos river and its tributary, the Therron, (known locally as the "*Rema tis Vlychias*") 15 kilometres long, which rises in Archanes and flows into the sea at Poros, east of Herakleion. The port of Knossos was situated at the mouth of the Kairatos - the area known today as Katsambas and Poros.

East of the hill where the palace was built, rises mount Ai-Lias, as it is known locally (the mountain of the Prophet Elijah), a long and narrow calcareous hill, 300 metres high, covered with olive groves on the lower part of its western slope. A strong ancient wall, probably a retaining wall, stands on the side facing the palace. The marly limestone rocks of the hill were used as building material for the palace. The quarries from which they have come are situated at the place called Spelia.

High up on the hill opposite the palace stands the church of Aghia Paraskevi, which was built on the site of a Byzantine church decorated with wall frescoes, mentioned by the 15th century traveller, Ch. Buondelmonti.

To the north of the Head is the low hill of Djafer Papoura, and the hill of the Venizeleion University of Crete, and to the south are situated the Upper and Lower Gypsades, composed in the higher parts of crystalline gypsum rocks which were used in the building of the palace. To the west is the Acropolis (Monastiriako Kefali). The lower slopes of these hills are of soft yellowish-white limestone, (locally known as "kouskous") exceptionally well-suited to the cultivation of olive trees and vines.

In the past few decades, with the use of machinery in farming, the natural environment of Knossos has undergone several changes. The waters of the Kairatos no longer flow throughout the year, as in antiquity. Cultivated areas were fewer then, and the higher parts of

the hills were covered with forests of cypress and oak.

The climate of Knossos is characteristically Mediterranean. The average rainfall in Herakleion, occurring mainly during the period between October and March, is 477 mm. The mean annual temperature ranges from 12° Celsius in January to 26° Celsius in July.

# HISTORY OF THE EXCAVATIONS

The first archaeological research, although amateur, as is natural, was conducted in 1878 by Minos Kalokairinos, a merchant from Herakleion, who uncovered the southern section of the western storerooms of the Palace.

He donated one each of the "pithoi" (large storage jars) which he discovered to the London, Paris, Rome and Athens museums. Also one to the Crown Prince of Greece, Constantine, and three to the collection of the Herakleion Educational Association, (the nucleus of the Cretan museum). The remainder of the finds he kept in his own home in

*The area of Knossos from the east, during the period of excavations by A. Evans.*

Herakleion, where they were destroyed during the 1898 uprising. The finds had, in the meantime, been published by the Frenchman Haussoulier and the German, Fabricius. The discoveries of Minos Kalokairinos stimulated the interest of many prospective diggers, who attempted to buy the area of the palace from its Turkish owners. These were the American Consul W.J. Stillman, Heinrich Schliemann, the excavator of Troy and of Mycenae, who came to Crete together with his collaborator W. Dörpfeld in 1886, and the French archaeologist M. Joubin. All of them were unsuccessful in their negotiations with the owners.

*SIR ARTHUR EVANS who excavated Knossos.*

The British archaeologist A.J. Evans was more successful. He bought the site and began digging in 1900, after the liberation of Crete from the Turks. He obtained permission to dig from the Cretan state and used his own funds for the excavation work. Within three years (1900-1902), the greater part of the palace had come to light.

In the following years, complementary excavations inside the palace were carried out, and the houses around the palace were uncovered, as well as the extensive burial grounds of Minoan Knossos. After a temporary halt between 1912-1922, the work was resumed until

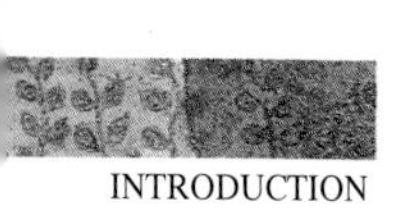

1931, when the "southern royal tomb" was discovered and excavated.

Apart from the excavation works, Sir Arthur Evans undertook the ambitious and important task of partially reconstructing and restoring the palace. A task, unique in so far as a large prehistoric monument is concerned, and one which he carried out with great daring, knowledge and imagination. Without Arthur Evans' restoration, our knowledge of the Minoan civilization would be very scant. Although he was much criticized - perhaps not entirely unjustly - for excesses, yet his restoration remained valuable and useful for many decades. We must not forget, of course, that it was undertaken 85 years ago, and that today other views on the subject of restoration of monuments prevail.

Sir Arthur Evans was assisted by several eminent archaeologists: D. Mackenzie, D. Ho-

*Restoration works at the Grand Staircase about 1910.*

garth, E. Forsdyke and H. Payne. Among his close collaborators were also the architects Th. Fyfe, Chr. Doll and F. Newton as well as the painters Gillieron father and son. It is to the latter that we owe the marvellous reconstitutions of the palace and of the palace frescoes.

Between 1921 and 1935, Sir Arthur Evans published his monumental, six-volume opus, *The Palace of King Minos at Knossos*, a work which constitutes the bible of Minoan archaeology. He also published many books and essays on Minoan Crete.

Few scholars have been so honoured during their lifetime as was Sir Arthur Evans, who died, at a ripe old age, in 1941.

Between 1930 and the Second World War, the archaeologists, J. Pendlebury, J. Brock and R. Hutchinson carried out excavations at Knossos, while, after the War, research on the

palace site and in the surrounding areas was continued by other British archaeologists led by S. Hood, the most authoritative living scholar on Minoan civilization, today. Hood conducted additional excavations in and around the palace, so as to confirm and complement the data concerning archaeological research at Knossos. Apart from his three general books on the Minoan civilization (see Bibliography), he drew accurate plans of the palace ruins and was in charge of the archaeological topographical charting of the Knossos area. Alongside S. Hood and after him, several eminent archaeologists carried out research at Knossos. The architect Piet de Jong drew several plans, J. Evans systematically studied the neolithic strata of the west and central courts of the palace. N. Coldstream excavated the sanctuary of Demeter at Gypsades and M. Gough the Villa Dionysus. M. Popham and H. Sackett uncovered the Unexplored Mansion by the Little Palace, Peter Warren dug along the "Royal Way" and south of the Villa Ariadne, G. Cadogan carried out excavations at several points within the palace area, while H. Catlin, R. Howel and J. Carrington-Smith dug up a section of the northern cemetery and a cemeterial basilica on the University campus. This research was recently resumed by C. Macdonald, west of the palace.

The number of archaeologists, both British and Greek involved in the excavations of Knossos exceeds fifty. During the past few decades rescue operations have been carried

out by the archaeologists of the Ephorate of Antiquities of Herakleion, A. Lebessis, A. Karetsou, N. Dimopoulou, A. Vassilakis, M. Bredaki, E. Grammatikaki, E. Banou, on plots of land at Knossos and at the northern cemetery in the area of the University of Crete, where several tombs, dating from 1100 BC. to 400 AD have been excavated.

The Knossos excavations, as is the case with all archaeological sites, also have their unseen protagonists. Here we shall mention, in order of seniority, the unforgettable skilled workmen and overseers: Manolis Akoumianakis, Manolis Markoyiannakis, Spyros A. Vassilakis, Antonis Zidianakis and the restorer Petros Petrakis. Let me be allowed to dedicate this book to their memory.

Sir Arthur Evans initially used as his "headquarters" the house of a Turkish bey, to the

southeast of the palace. Later he built the Villa Ariadne which he himself and the British School of Archaeology used until 1952, when it was ceded to the Greek state. Since then, the British School is housed in the buildings of the "Taverna" of the Villa Ariadne, while the finds from both the older and the more recent excavations are kept in the Stratigraphic Museum, which was built in 1964, south of the Villa Ariadne.

During the last decade before the Second World War, the Ephor of Antiquities, Nikolaos Platon undertook much consolidation and restoration work as well as additional research. within and around the palace. The work was continued, in the first decades after the war, by Platon and by the Ephor of Antiquities, Stylianos Alexiou.

In 1976, by Presidential Decree, the erection of buildings in the area was only allowed within the limits of the existing settlements and a very broad space was defined in which construction was prohibited, so as to protect the unique archaeological site of Knossos.

In the 1980s, a programme began to be set up for the consolidation and conservation of the palace structures which had started to show signs of considerable wear. The route to be followed by visitors was also defined. These works are now in progress; when they are completed and the parking areas to the north of the Palace properly laid out, the appearance of the site will be substantially improved and the flow of visitors greatly facilitated.

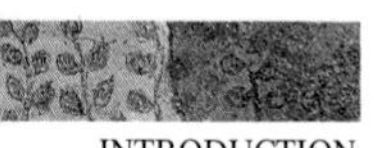



# MYTHS AND LEGENDS
## ASSOCIATED WITH KNOSSOS

*Europa and Zeus in the shape of a Bull. From a red-figure vase.*

The plot and action of many ancient Greek myths are set on Crete, and revolve around the king of Knossos, Minos, son of Zeus and of Europa, the Phoenician nymph.
Minos, together with his brothers Rhadamanthys and Sarpedon, was born on Crete, at Gortyn, and was adopted by the King of Crete, Asterius who married Europa and made Minos his heir to the throne. Minos married Pasiphae, daughter of Helios, the sun-god, and of the nymph, Crete. Of this marriage were born four sons and four daughters,Catreus, Xenodike, Ariadne, Androgeus, Glaucus, Deucalion, Phaedra and Acalle (or Acaccalis).
Several dramatic mythical events took place at the palace of Knossos. As the myth relates, Minos received as a gift

from Poseidon an extraordinarily handsome white bull, which he undertook to sacrifice to the god. Minos however failed to fulfill his promise and, in order to punish him, Poseidon instilled a passionate love for the bull in the heart of Pasiphae. At the palace, in those days, there lived a marvellously skilled craftsman named Daedalus, who, in compliance with Pasiphae's wish, created for her a carved wooden image of a cow covered with real hide, in which the queen hid and thus mated with the divine bull. From their union was born the

*Left: Representation of Theseus and the Minotaur on a black-figure vase.*

*Above:*
*The Minotaur on a silver coin from Knossos (5th century BC).*

Minotaur, a man with the head of a bull, who was also named Asterius, and who was imprisoned by Minos in the maze-like building, the Labyrinth, created by Daedalus.

One of the sons of Minos, Androgeus, was killed in Athens, after having won a contest in the Athenian games. His murder was the cause of Minos' imposing on the Athenians the obligation to send seven youths and seven maidens every ninth year, to be devoured by the Minotaur. This is where the Athenian hero, Theseus - who, according to one legend, was a son of Poseidon - comes into the myth. Theseus offered himself as one of the victime to be sent to Crete. There, Ariadne fell in love with him and, together with Daedalus, helped him enter the Labyrinth and kill the Minotaur, thus putting an end to the tribute of blood. Theseus left Crete together with his companions and with Ariadne whom, in compliance with the will of the gods, he abandoned on the

island of Naxos, ceding her to Dionysus. From the union of Dionysus and Ariadne were born Staphylos, Thoas and Oenopion.

The myth of prince Glaucus is also a colourful one. Glaucus was being initiated into the art of divination by Polyeidos, the seer from Argos. As the young prince was playing in the palace one day, he fell into a jar used for storing honey and drowned. King Minos ordered Polyeidos to bring him back to life and locked them both up in an underground chamber. Polyeidos managed to restore Glaucus to life by using a herb brought to him by a serpent. After this, the seer taught Glaucus his art but, when he was leaving to return to his country, Argos, and was about to embark, he asked Glaucus to spit into his mouth, whereupon Glaucus lost all his divinatory powers.

The mythological cycle closes with the dramatic flight of Daedalus and his son Icarus from Crete, with waxen wings made by Daedalus himself. The wax having melted, Icarus fell into the sea, - the Icarian Sea - and was drowned. Daedalus sought refuge in Sicily, where he was pursued by king Minos. With the help of a Sicilian princess, however, and of king Cocalus, he managed to escape but Minos was killed. He was buried with great pomp by his followers in Sicily, where the town of Minoa was founded in his honour. After his death, both he and his brother Rhadamanthys were deified and became divine judges of souls in Hades, together with Aeacus, the grandfather of Achilles.

*Theseus and Ariadne. Representation on a vase from Arkades. (Archaeological Museum of Herakleion).*

Another famous king of Crete was Idomeneus, grandson of Minos, and son of Deucalion. Idomeneus took part in the Trojan War, where he distinguished himself and was the third strongest and bravest of the Greek leaders. Idomeneus personifies the dynamism of Crete during the Mycenean period.

As is the case with all myths, those of Knossos do not themselves constitute history, but they do conceal, in their core, certain historical facts. Thus, Ariadne, the young heroine from Knossos who dies on the island of Dia, now known as Naxos, is the personification of the young goddess of fruitful growth who dies and is reborn each year, following the cycle of nature.

The mythical labyrinth is the palace of Knossos itself, with its uniquely intricate layout, while in the personality of Daedalus we find condensed the essence of the technological evolution and

progress of the Minoans. The story about the Athenian youths and maidens who were offered up to the Minotaur, awakens echoes of the famous "taurokathapsia" (bull-leaping), of which the Minoans were very fond, but it also indicates the influence exercised by Knossos over the entire southern part of Greece all the way to Athens. Europa, to whom our continent owes its name, was the mother of the divine Minos, who gave his name to the first European civilization. Minos may have been the title of the kings of Knossos, as "Pharaoh" was that of the Egyptian kings, or there may have been one or more kings of the same name. What is more important is that, in the figure of Minos, the ancient Greeks saw a powerful ruler, an inspired law-giver, an equitable judge, the sovereign of the largest portion of the Greek world, during the period when the Minoan civilization was at its peak.

# HISTORY

*Knossos, on Crete, was one of the most ancient cities of the Aegean and of Europe.*

*The vast site over which the ruins lie, at a distance of approximately 5 kilometres from Herakleion, the modern capital of Crete, is visited every day by thousands of people from all over the world. They come to see and to admire the remains of this brilliant and refined ancient Greek civilization. There has been a constant human presence on this site for about eight thousand years, from 6000 BC to our day.*

*This long course of mankind in this favoured corner of the earth we shall now follow in a brief narration.*

# CHRONOLOGICAL TABLE

**NEOLITHIC PERIOD (7000-3500 BC)**

**BRONZE AGE (3500-1000 BC)**
Prepalatial period (3500-1900 BC)
Old Palace period (1900-1700/1650 BC)
New Palace period (1700/1650-1450 BC)
Third Palace period (1450-1350/1300 BC)
Postpalatial period (1350/1300-1100 BC)
Subminoan period (1100-1000 BC)

**EARLY IRON AGE (1000-67 BC)**
Protogeometric period (1000-800 BC)
Geometric period (800-700 BC)
Early Archaic (Orientalizing) period (700-650 BC)
High Archaic period (650-500 BC)
Classical period (500-330 BC)
Hellenistic period (330-67 BC)

**GRECO-ROMAN PERIOD (67 BC-323 AD)**
**EARLY BYZANTINE PERIOD (323-824)**
**ARAB DOMINATION (824-961)**
**BYZANTINE PERIOD (961-1204)**
**PERIOD OF VENETIAN RULE (1204-1669)**
**PERIOD OF TURKISH RULE (1669-1898)**

***Note:***
*The chronology proposed here-apart from certain small variations-is in accord with that proposed by G. Cadogan 1992 (See bibliography).*

# HISTORICAL DEVELOPMENT

## THE NEOLITHIC AGE (CIRCA 5700-2800 B.C.)

The low hill of Knossos was first inhabited shortly after 6000 BC. Within three thousand years it had become the largest Neolithic settlement on Crete and one of the largest and most important of Greece.

The Neolithic strata have been fully and systematically explored and we thus have a good deal of information on the life of the people of that period. Within a very short time, taking advantage of the stability which prevailed in the area after the last Ice Age, the inhabitants of Neolithic Knossos developed a mixed economy based on agriculture and animal husbandry.

They were also adept in handicrafts. The clay pottery they produced, after their initial trials, was created with astonishing artistry. Stone tools were constantly being improved, while animal bones and horns were also used to

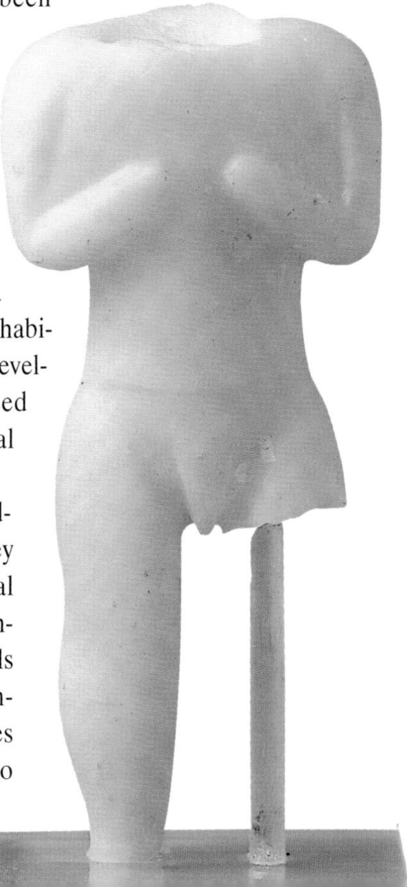

*Marble figurine of a man. 6.500-5.800 BC. (Archaeological Museum of Herakleion).*

make the implements that were necessary to them. Interesting, too are the clay or stone figurines, representing male and female forms. The houses built by the inhabitants of Knossos, and composed of small rooms around a larger, central room, were made of mud bricks, dried in the sun and set on stone foundations. The area of the Neolithic settlement, around 3000 BC, was approximately the same as that of the later palace.

*Axes of the Neolothic period (Archaeological Museum of Herakleion).*

Below the central court of the palace, were found the Mesolithic strata. The Neolithic strata of Knossos have only partially survived. This is due to the extensive re-use and levelling of the ruins of the Neolithic settlement when the first palace came to be built.

The Neolithic period at Knossos, coincided with a relatively advanced stage of civilization. The knowledge and use of metals, and primarily of bronze, marks the beginning of the next stage of civilization.

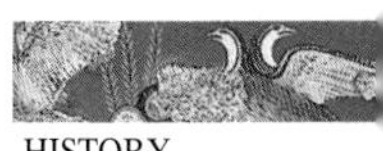



## THE BRONZE AGE
## (CIRCA 2800 - 1000 B. C.)

This period, which lasted approximately 2000 years, was the first great and brilliant period of Cretan civilization, and indeed, of the entire Greek world. In Crete, during these centuries, was born, grew, evolved and reached its culmination the first Greek cultural miracle of the Aegean world, the Minoan civilization. The development of this civilization can be divided into four periods, distinguished by the key events of its historical course, such as the foundation, destruction, reconstruction and final devastation of the palace.

The periods, are those proposed by Professor N. Platon, in 1959. Also used, especially in dating pottery, is the system devised by Sir Arthur Evans):

*Clay pyxis decorated with an incised design. Early Bronze Age, 3rd millenium BC. (Herakleion Museum).*

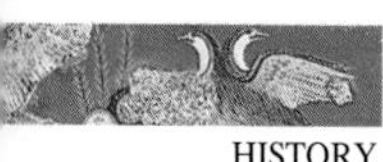



## The Prepalatial Period (3500-1900 BC.)

Visitors to Knossos do not see the ruins of the Prepalatial period, since these were levelled in order to erect the great palace.

However, we know from the excavations carried out , that a large prepalatial settlement existed here. Houses belonging to this settlement were uncovered at a deep level, to the north and south of the Royal Way, in the area of the West Court and under the West Magazines of the palace.

The most important building, perhaps the centre of the settlement, an "early palace", has been found under the northeastern and northern sections of the later palace.

Also of the same period are the large underground chambers and the large "basement", a hewn construction, which had been used as a storeroom or cistern and which lies under the southern façade of the palace. It is figured that the settlement extended westwards as far as the "acropolis" and northwards as far as the present settlement of Makrys Toichos.

Excavation of the prepalatial settlement is difficult because of the existence of more recent buildings on the site. However, the finds that have come to light indicate that, already at that time, Knossos was in contact with the Cyclades, with continental Greece and with Egypt.

*Clay tablet with Linear A script (Archaeological Museum, Herakleion).*

## The Period Of The Old Palace (1900-1700/1650 BC)

*Kamares-style vessel dated to around 1800 BC (Archaeological Museum of Herakleion).*

The foundation of the palace at Knossos, as is the case with that of the other Cretan centres, was an event of the highest historical, political, economic and social importance, and the natural development and consequence of the economic and cultural flowering which took place towards the end of the previous period.

The palaces were the centre of all the life and activities of the city-state. In them were stored and kept, under the protection of the deity, the agricultural produce and the livestock, in which the palace traded.

Here, too, in separate areas, were workshops where were created the wonderful pottery, stonework, small artifacts and jewellery we see today. The palace was not only the residence of the members of the royal family, but also that of a numerous administrative and religious hierarchy.

The conditions under which the palaces were created are not completely clear. Very little has survived of the old palace of Knossos, owing to the fact that on its site was built the new palace. Its dimensions and plan, with its

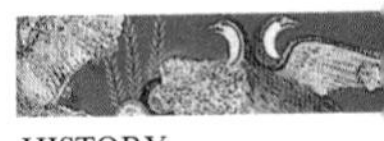



two large courts, may have been the same as those of the later palace. Today, it is believed that it constituted a single building complex. Sir Arthur Evans, on the other hand, had put forward the theory of the *insulae*, that is of independent large buildings which were gradually linked together. The palace appears to have been built in two stages. During the second construction stage, was laid out the paved west court in which were sunk the "kouloures", the walled circular pits which served as granaries or rubbish depositories, over the ruins of the houses of the previous stage. These pits were covered during the period of the new palace.

Generally speaking, we are now fairly certain that the magazines and shrines, as well as the administrative offices (depositories of tablets inscribed with ideograms) were located in the west wing, which also housed the shrines and storerooms of the newer palace. In the northeastern sector were the pottery work-

*The circular walled depositories ("kouloures") in the west court of the Palace.*

*Rhyton in the shape of a bull's head. Steatite. From the Small Palace, circa 1550-1500 BC. (Archaeological Museum of Herakleion).*

shops, where the polychrome Kamares ware was produced, and the royal magazines which contained the giant *pithoi* (storage jars) we can still see today.

Around the palace were built retaining walls, and there was an enclosure on the western side. Very little is known about the city of the old palace period, although it is certain that it was already large and extensive.

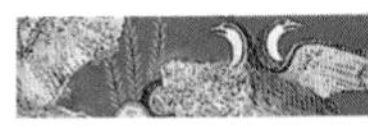



The Royal Way and the West Court were perhaps paved during this period. The large viaduct to the south of the palace also dates from this period. The cemeteries of the city were situated on the slopes of the Ai-Lias hill. They consisted of cave-tombs and contained a great many pithos burials.

Despite the lack of very much evidence related to the Knossos of this period, it was already the centre of one of the great domains that took shape in Crete at that time (the others being those of Phaestos and Malia). These domains were linked between themselves and were also in contact with the centres of the Aegean, of the East and of Egypt.

However we cannot as yet speak of a sovereign position of Knossos, as regards all of Crete. The area of the city during the old palace period is not known, but it seems to have extended as far as the hill of the acropolis. Its cemeteries have been excavated on the slopes of Ai Lias and on the hill of Gypsades, to the south. It is difficult to say a great deal concerning life in the Knossos of that period. We do not know whether it was of a religious character or whether – as is more likely – the mundane element was predominant. With the arrival of the next period, it is the religious element that will prevail.

*Prochous with a floral decoration of reeds. Circa 1550-1500 BC (Archaeological Museum of Herakleion).*

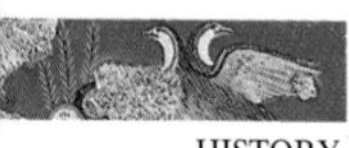



## The Period Of The New Palace (1700/1650 - 1450 BC).

The old palace was completely destroyed around 1700 BC, after it had twice previously suffered partial destruction. The problem of how and why this destruction occurred is a complex one. Usually this kind of devastation is attributed to natural phenomena, such as earthquakes and fires.

The new palace was built according to a new set of plans, since the hilltop was levelled again and the palace erected on the fill. A deep cutting was also made on the eastern side of the hill, and on the lower level, eight metres down, which was thus formed, were built the royal apartments of the east wing. The new palace covered a total area of 22,000 sq. metres (or about 5,5 acres). This palace also was de-

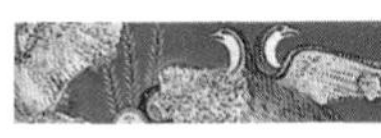

*The "Customs House" and the North Entrance.*

stroyed three times. The greater part of the ruins which are visible today belong to the second phase of the new palace (1600-1500 BC). During the next phases several changes were made to parts of the palace, but these did not significantly alter its general structure. They will be referred to later in special chapters of this guide. Here, only the general picture presented to the viewer by the palace 3500 years before our time will be given, as well as its basic and characteristic features.

One could enter the palace of Knossos through any one of five entrances: the northern one, the southern one, the northwestern one, the southwestern one and the eastern one. The first four were the more formal entrances, with propyla and wide portals. To the west of the palace extended the paved west court, traversed by processional ways. In this area two altars had been built.

In the southwestern corner of the court was the western entrance. It had a columned

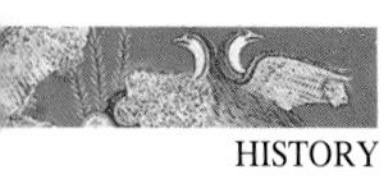



propylon and led, from the south, along a wide processional corridor in the shape of the Greek letter Π, to the central court, at the spot where the reproduction of the fresco of the "priest prince" can be seen today.

There was another monumental entrance to the south (great propylaea). This was where the stepped portico, which led from the guest house to the south across the viaduct, ended up. From the great propylaea a grand staircase led to the first floor of the west wing (*piano nobile*). This wing had large ceremonial rooms on the upper floor. On the ground floor were situated the magazines, the shrines, the treasuries and the throne room.

In the northern section were the magazines, a "lustral area" which has been restored today, and the "Customs House". On either side of a ramp leading from the Customs House to the central court there were impressive porches, one of which, adorned with a bull in relief, has been restored. Outside the northwestern corner of the palace was situated the "theatre" built of stone, where ended the "Royal Way" which passed through the city from the north-

*Clay tablet with Linear B script. From the "Mycenean Palace" of Knossos. (Herakleion Museum).*

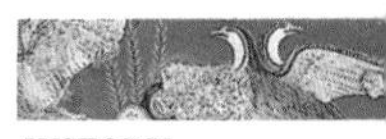



west. The “royal apartments” were situated in the east wing. To the north of these, were the workshops and to the south a shrine. Some of the houses in the southeastern corner, outside the palace, have been excavated.

## The Minoan City And Its Cemeteries

During the Neopalatial period, Knossos was at the height of its splendour. Around the palace, mainly to the west and north, but also in the lower parts of the hills of the Acropolis and Gypsades, lay the city with the large houses for the priests, the officials and the middle class. All of these were grand and impressive in construction, and adorned with beautiful frescoes.

According to Sir Arthur Evans, the town, extended over an area of 1250 *stremmata*. Its population he estimated at 80-100,000 inhabitants (though these numbers seem rather exaggerated). Other figures, proposed by S. Hood, according to whom the area of Minoan Knossos was 750 *stremmata* and its population 15-20,000, seem a more realistic estimate.

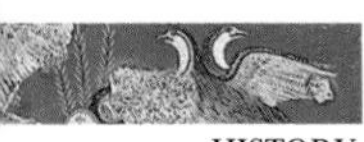



The harbour of Knossos constituted part of the great city (Evans calls it a "port city"). It was situated where the eastern quarters of Herakleion, Poros - Katsamba are today. The port proper was situated at the site of Trypiti (The area is greatly altered today, owing to the construction of the extension of the new port and the coastal avenue). On the level land where the Kairatos flows out into the sea, stood the houses of the rich merchants and seamen of Knossos. Their tombs, where many funeral gifts were found, were cut into the hill-sides. During the past decades, important finds have been uncovered in houses and tombs.

The cemeteries of Knossos extend in every direction, on the hillsides and as far as the modern suburb of Aghios Ioannis, two and a half kilometres north of the palace. Most of the tombs are rock-cut chamber tombs, but there were also some monumental tombs, such as the southern royal grave-shrine at Gypsa-des, the royal tomb at Isopata (destroyed by vandals during the German occupation), the tholos tombs at Kefala and Gypsades.

Much of the road network of the ancient city is not known to us. The "Royal Way", which follows a northwesterly direction, has been un-covered, as well as a portion of its extension in the area west of the Stratigraphical Museum. Unlike what has been the case at other Minoan sites, at Knossos we are unable to say what the town plan was like, since none of the quarters of the city has been excavated in its entirety.

The irrigation and drainage system at

Knossos is most interesting. The aqueduct conveyed water from a great distance (from the Kounavoi and Archanes areas) through tubular conduits, and branched out inside the city and the palace, where parts of the drainage system have been found.

There were two built drainage channels, one to collect the sewage and the other the rain water, which passed through the palace and carried the water outside.

This was the period when the palace and the city were at the height of their glory. The inhabitants of Knossos, like all the Minoans, lived happily on their blessed land. They worshipped the Mother Goddess in her shrines, in homes and out of-doors. Their carts and pack animals carried produce to the palace and the port. Their ships sailed back and forth across the seas, over which Crete reigned supreme, and carried her products to every part of the known world. In exchange, they brought back to the island many raw materials.

*Pithoi from the south propylaea of the Palace.*

## The "Mycenean" Palace (1450-1350 BC)

This happy life in the palace and in the city was rudely shattered by a natural phenomenon, known from the past.

Around 1450 BC, according to the most prevalent theory, all the palatial cities of Crete were destroyed by an earthquake and fire which had previously been believed to have been caused by the eruption of the volcano of Santorini. The latest theory, however, is that the devastation was the result of enemy action. The palace managed to withstand the shock and went on living, after some repairs and alterations, for another 70 to 100 years, until 1380/1350 BC.

Our knowledge concerning this last phase in the life of the palace of Knossos, is mainly based on archaeological evidence (pottery and architecture), but also on the tablets inscribed in Linear B script which were found in the palace. The main conclusion is that a Mycenean *anax* (king) had installed himself in the palace of Knossos, which was, during this period, the only palatial centre in Crete. We do not know under what circumstances this dynastic change took place. It has been attributed to military conquest, to peaceful intermarriage or to a coup by a Mycenean general of the Minoan navy. It is a fact, in any case, that the Myceneans took advantage of the shock which followed the disaster to establish themselves at Knossos. Various alterations were then made

to the palace: the throne room was incorporated into the old structure and adorned with frescoes in which the Mycenean influence is apparent. In pottery, the Mycenean inlfuence is even more evident (Palace style). The language which was written and spoken was the Mycenean dialect of the Greek language. The general spirit was militaristic, in obvious contrast to that of the peace-loving Minoans. Burials of warriors took place at Knossos (in the Venizeleion Hospital area of today).

The *anax* of Knossos was the overlord of the entire island. From clay tablets we know the names of the cities which were under the control of Knossos: Amnissos and Tylissos, Phaestos and Inatos, Lyktos, Lato, Siteia and Itanos,

*The Throne Room with the unique stone throne and gypsum benches. (c. 1450-1350 BC).*

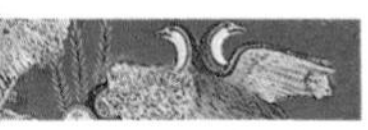



Sybritos, Kydonia and Aptera. They raised herds of sheep and sent the wool to the palace. Commerce was once again in the hands of the king, as in previous years. Relations with Egypt and with the rest of the known world were close.

Everyday life remained basically purely Minoan. The Myceneans were satisfied with retaining suzerainty over the island. Religion, too, remained Minoan, although new divinities were introduced.

*Vase of the Orientalising period.*

THE POST-PALATIAL PERIOD

Around 1380/1300 BC a new disaster befell Knossos. Some scholars date it to the end of the 14th or the beginning of the 13th centrury (a little before or after 1300 BC). Its causes are not entirely known. The fire which devastated the palace has been attributed to an accidental cause or to a revolt of the subjugated Minoans, or even to an uprising of the Myceneans of Knossos against the Myceneans who came from mainland Greece, that brought about the final obliteration of Mycenean Knossos, which until then had still been powerful. Whatever the cause may have been, the majority of scholars agree that the palace of Knossos ceased to

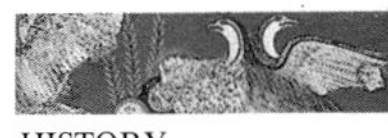



exist - at least in the form in which we know it - after these disastrous events. In the years which followed, the ruins of the palace were for a time "reoccupied" by private individuals, who brought about certain alterations to various parts of the structure. The southern propylaea were used as storerooms and a pottery workshop was installed in the queen's megaron.

In the Homeric epics, which are usually considered to be a source of information on the later phase of the Minoan and Mycenean periods, the personage of Idomeneus is mentioned as being king of Knossos and of Crete. The problem of where Idomeneus' seat was established remains unsolved. If we accept that this was at Mycenean Knossos, we must also accept that the palace was standing here until the second half of the 13th century BC.

The splendid Minoan palace, after six centuries of grandeur, ended up as a desolate ruin. Only the ghosts of its old glory remained, to haunt the ruined staircases and passages, the megara and shrines, to mourn the brilliant past. It was perhaps the extent and impressive intricacy of the ruins of the magnificent palace which gave birth to the myth of the Labyrinth.

*Vase with marine style decoration.*

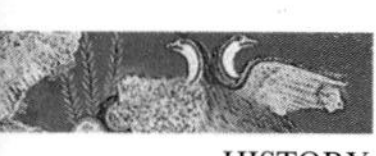



## THE "CITY-STATE" OF KNOSSOS

### THE EARLY IRON AGE
### THE ARCHAIC PERIOD (1000-500 BC)

Bronze Age Knossos was succeeded, on the same site, by the city-state of Knossos, which lasted approximately 1000 years. The palace area was considered sacred and the ruins were not inhabited. According to the historian, Diodorus, it was then a sacred wood in which stood a small temple dedicated to the goddess Rhea.

Now the nucleus of the city was situated to the north and west of the site of the old palace, near which there were three temples or shrines: that of Demeter at Gypsades, that of Rhea on the palace site itself, and that of Zeus and Hera on the so-called acropolis. Not known is the location of the seat of the local king or lord and that of the city's agora. Better known are the extensive cemeteries in the area of the Venizeleion and the University, and still further to the north.

It is estimated that the city covered an area of 500-600 *stremmata* (1 *stremma* = 1000 sq. metres) and had a corresponding number of inhabitants. It was probably organized as a number of large villages dependent on a central town, situated to the west and north of the palace.

The cultural and artistic influence of Knossos extended throughout the island, in which it held the position of metropolis. Knossos' relations with the other important centres in Greece and the East were also very close.

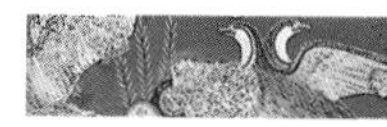



## The Classical And Hellenistic Periods

Knossos was one of the most important cities in Crete, a friend and ally alternately of the other important cities of Gortyn, Lyktos and Kydonia. Only a few ruins dating from these four centuries are known to us.

In the southwestern part of the area of the "Villa Ariadne", and to the west of the present settlement, at the foot of the acropolis, were situated potters' workshops. Of the sanctuar-

*Metope of a temple with a representation of Heracles and the Erymanthian Boar.*

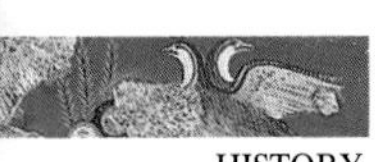



ies of the previous period, still in use were the temple of Demeter at Gypsades, the temple of Rhea on the palace site, the shrine-heroön of Glaucus in today's settlement of Bougada Metochi, two temples on the "acropolis", identified with the temple of Zeus and Hera, and the temple of the Apollo Delphinius as well as one more temple in the area known today as "Tekés". Few are the structural remains of sanctuaries and temples, but certain inscriptions and architectural elements (metopes, cornices etc.) have been discovered.

## THE GRECO-ROMAN PERIOD

During the 2nd and the beginning of the 1st century BC, Knossos was the proud and powerful Cretan city which stood up to the Roman conqueors. This resistance cost her her undisputed,until then, preeminent position in Crete. A position which, after the Roman conquest of 67 BC, was occupied by Gortyn.

Knossos was now a Roman "colony". It covered an area of approximately 500-600 stremmata. It was, however, a flourishing city with splendid public buildings and private houses. Their ruins are still to be seen today at the site now known as Hellenika, between the Venizeleion Hospital and the "Villa Ariadne". The mosaics of the "Villa Dionysus" are among the best of the Roman Imperial period.

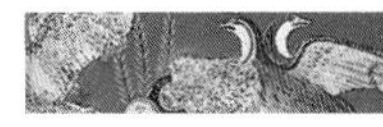



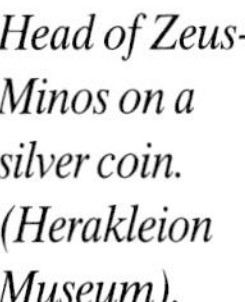

*Head of Zeus-Minos on a silver coin. (Herakleion Museum).*

Sections of a large aqueduct of Roman times have been uncovered at Spelia, south of Knossos and many graves of a variety of types dating to this period have been excavated, from simple, tile-covered graves to rock-cut chamber tombs, and underground or ground-level mausolea. One such mausoleum that has not survived was that known as “Caiaphas’ grave”, which was studied by S. Xanthoudides.

*The Labyrinth pictured on a silver coin. (Herakleion Museum).*

Other Roman mausolea preserved by the northern entrance of the University and between that and the Hospital were recently excavated by the present writer and other archaeologists.

## THE FIRST BYZANTINE PERIOD

In the early centuries of Christianity, Knossos was an important centre and a bishop's see. Three of its churches, of the basilica type have been studied by archaeologists: one decorated with mosaics in the area of the Venizeleion Hospital, a second one in the Makrys Toichos settlement, where the church of Aghia Sophia stands today, and a third one, a cemetery church, on the University grounds.

At some point in time, before the 9th century AD, the see was transferred to Raukos, to the site of the present village of Aghios Myronas Maleviziou. The administrative centre was also transferred to its seaport, Herakleion. The city gradually shrank to a small village, on the site of the present village of Makrys Toichos.

## THE PERIOD OF ARAB DOMINATION - THE BYZANTINE PERIOD - THE PERIOD OF VENETIAN RULE

At the time of the Arab conquest, only a few huts stood on the site of the settlement of Makrys Toichos. In the middle Byzantine period and during the period of Venetian rule, there was a settlement around the church on the site of the basilica of Aghia Sophia. This is perhaps the church mentioned by Buondelmonti, or, according to another view, he may have been referring to the Byzantine church of

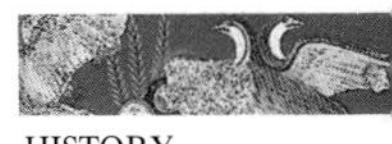



Aghia Paraskevi at Ai-Lias. He also mentions the "grave of Caiaphas" who, according to a local legend, was buried in Knossos. During the Venetian period, the settlement of Makrys Toichos was recorded as having 150 inhabitants.

## THE PERIOD OF OTTOMAN OCCUPATION

The small village of Makrys Toichos was renamed by the Turks Bougada Metochi, after the Bougada river (Tchamashir Déré) - the ancient Kairatos.

The name "Bougada", which means the "wash", is owed to the fact that the Turks of the Fortetsa military camp used to do their washing here, during the siege of the town of Candia (Herakleion).

At the end of the 19th century (1881), a number of small settlements or "metochia" (monastery dependencies) had been registered in the area of ancient Knossos: Hellenika to the north, Makrys Toichos to the northeast and Metochia to the west and south of the palace hill. The Makrys Toichos settlement is the oldest in the area, and its church (Aghia Sophia) is built on the site of an early Christian basilica. It owes its name to a long wall at Hellenika and Topana, which may have been part of a large building of Roman times. Makrys Toichos and the metochia had a population of 154 inhabitants (65 Christians and 89 Muslims). After 1900, the new settlement of

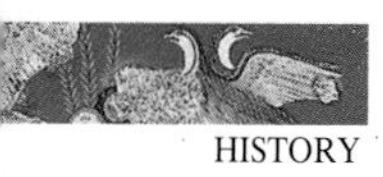

Knossos, west of the palace, reverted to its old name of Bougada Metochi. The metochi south of the palace, on the eastern flank of Gypsades, was named Vlychia, from the brackish spring of the same name that welled from the site of the Minoan guest house but which ran dry a few years ago.

## KNOSSOS IN THE 20TH CENTURY

The metochia later came under the jurisdiction of the Municipality of Herakleion, and its ancient name was revived, although the old names were not forgotten. In the early part of our century. Evans carried out his extensive excavations which changed the fate of the site and of the entire island. Evans' first "headquarters" were in a *konak*, a large house, to the

*Engraving of Candia (Herakleion), (Benaki Museum, Athens).*

southeast of the palace hill. Later, the Villa Ariadne - known to the locals as "the Villa"- was built to serve as the central office of the archaeological mission of Knossos. In 1952 the villa was ceded to the Greek State and in May 1941, during the Battle of Crete, the Greek king, George, and the Tsouderos government used the Villa Ariadne as their base for a short time.

One of the confrontations between the German forces and the people of Crete took place around Knossos. During the German Occupation, the High Command of the German forces in Crete made the Villa Ariadne their headquarters. It was here that the surrender of Germany to the victorious Allies was signed, in 1945. Today, the steady population of about 400 inhabitants, is involved in farming and tourism.

# HOW TO USE THIS GUIDE

*1.* The following symbols have been used on the maps and plans which accompany the text:

The capital letters A-L define the functional units of the palace.

The numbers 1-40 identify the most important rooms or areas of the palace.

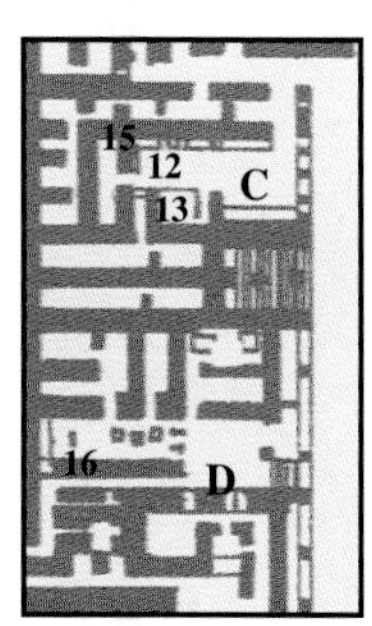


*2.* Most of the names of the various areas were established by the archaeologist, Sir Arthur Evans and are conventional, not always corresponding to their actual function. However, they have been used here for the sake of consistency with other texts and with the indicative signs within the archaeological site.

*3.* The areas of the palace which are closed for reasons of safety and protection are accessible only to scholars and researchers having obtained special permission from the Directorate of the Archaeological Services in Herakleion.

The closed areas around the palace can only be seen by visitors accompanied by the responsible custodian and guide.

*4.* The route which is suggested here for visiting the palace and the surrounding houses takes approximately two hours. To visit the outlying areas, a further hour and the use of a car are necessary.

# PALACE

A. WEST COURT
B. WEST MAGAZINES
C. THRONE ROOM SYSTEM
D. CENTRAL SHRINE SYSTEM
E. CENTRAL COURT
F. ROYAL APARTMENTS
G. SHRINE OF THE DOUBLE AXES
H. WORKSHOP AREA
I. GREAT EAST HALL
J. NORTH ENTRANCE SYSTEM
K. NORTH WESTERN SECTOR
L. THEATRAL AREA

1. "Kouloures" (Pits)
2. Altars
3. "Processional Way"
4. West Entrance
5. Corridor of the Procession
6. South Propylaeum
7. Large Stairease
8. Ceremonial Hall
9. Magazines
10. West Stairway
11. Anteroom
12. Throne Room
13. Lustral Area
14. Tripartite Shrine
15. "Treasury of the Central Shrine"
16. Pillar Crypt
17. Precinct of the Temple of Rhea
18. South Entrance
19. Grand Staircase

20-21. Hall of the Double Axes or Kings Megaron

22. Queen's Megaron
23. Bench-altar
24. Lustral Area
25. Stone cutters Workshop
26. Potter's Workshop
27. Court of the Stone Spout
28. Magazines of the Giant Pithoi
29. East Entrance
30. Magazine of the Pihtoi

31-32. Corridor of the Bays

33. Corridor of the Draughtboard
34. Magazines of the Old Palace
35. Northeastern sector
36. "Customs House"
37. North Entrance
38. Northern Lustral Area
39. Deep underground rooms
40. Theatral Area

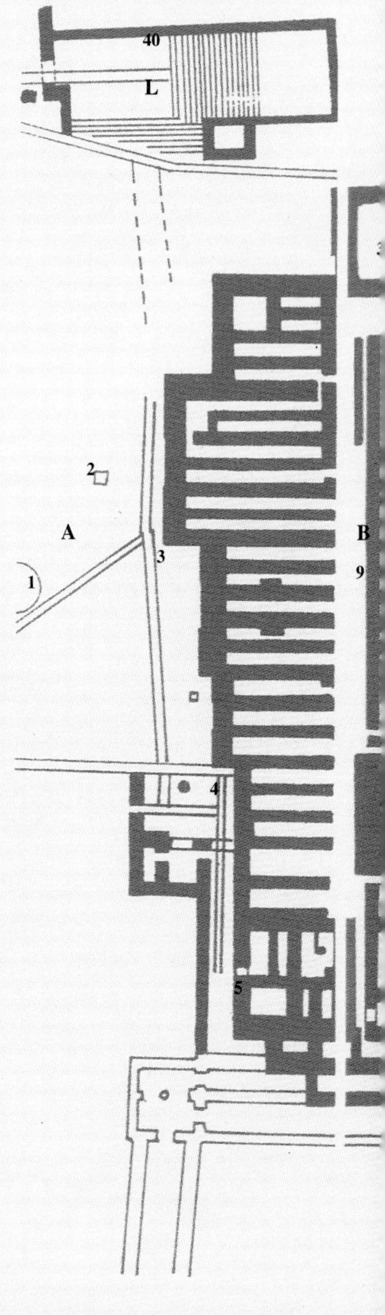

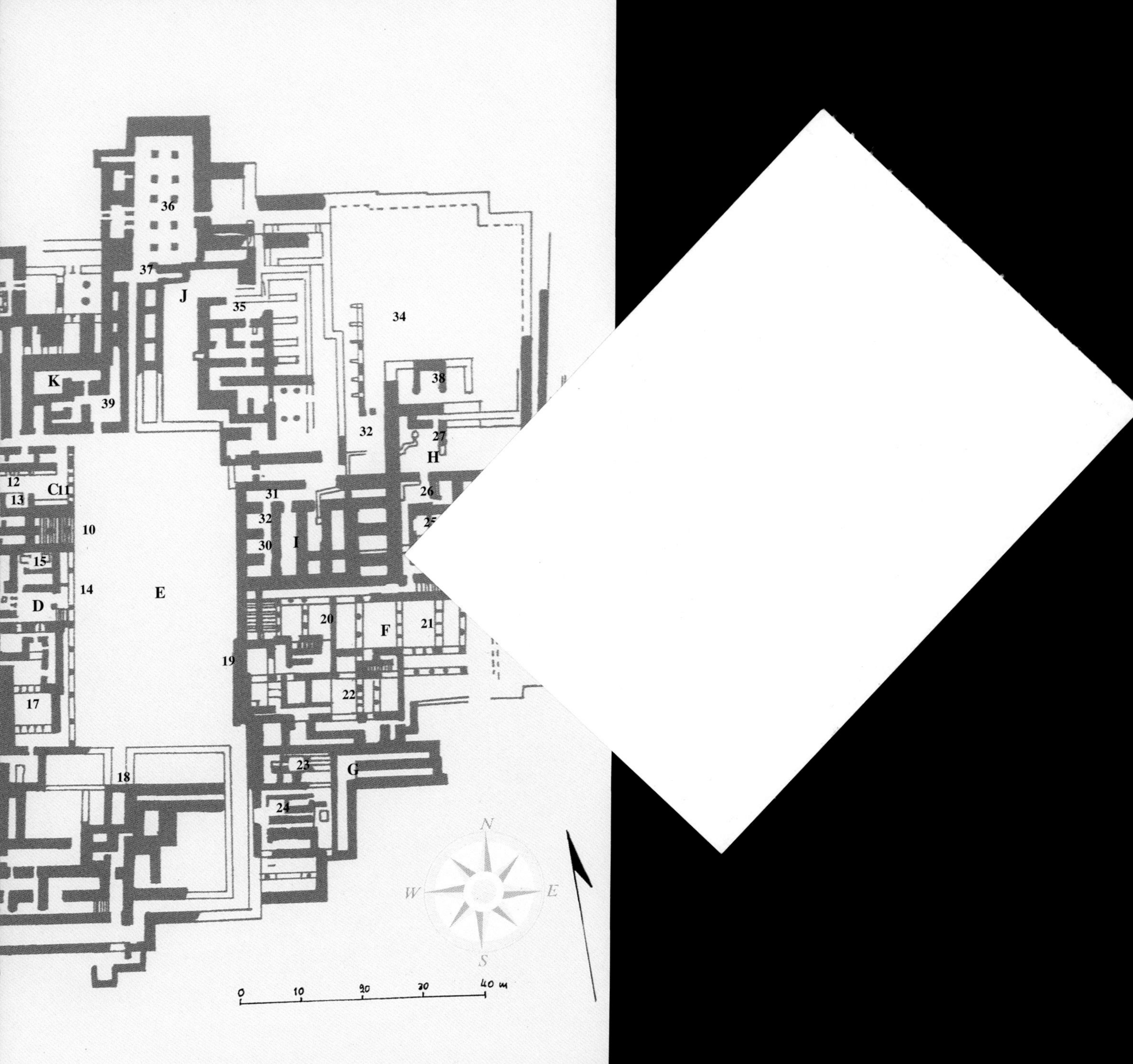

36
37
J
35
34
K
39
38
32
27
H
12
C11
13
31
26
10
32
30
I
15
14
E
D
20
F
21
19
22
17
23
G
18
24
N
W
E
S
0
10
20
30
40 m

ΤΑΠ ΤΑΠ ΤΑΠ ΤΑΠ ΤΑΠ ΤΑΠ
Ανάκτορο Κνωσού. Η αίθουσα του θρόνου. 1450-1400
Palace of Knossos. Throne Room. 1450-1400 BC.
ΑΛΕΞΑΝΔΡΟΣ ΜΑΤΣΟΥΚΗΣ Α.Ε.
ΚΝ
1846356
Παρακαλείσθε να κρατήσετε το απόκομμα του εισιτηρίου σας μέχρι την έξοδό σας από το Μουσείο/Χώρο.
You are requested to preserve your ticket, until you leave the Museum/Site
ΕΙΣΙΤΗΡΙΟ ΕΙΣΟΔΟΥ
ΕΥΡΩ 6 EURO
ENTRANCE TICKET

# GUIDE

*Knossos is one of the major archaeological sites in Greece in terms of its importance and interest to the visitor. This is because the mighty city of Minos and Ariadne, of Pasiphae, the Minotaur and Idomeneus, was undoubtedly one of the earliest cities on European soil, a centre which radiated the brilliance of one of the most splendid civilizations of Greek and European prehistory - the Minoan civilization, named after the great god-king Minos. The ruins of this city, partially restored by Sir Arthur Evans, stand as irrefutable witnesses of its ancient glory.*

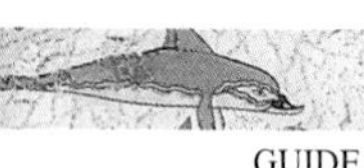



# VISITOR'S GUIDE
## KNOSSOS

The itinerary suggested by this guide is the one most commonly used and is the most practical and logical. However, if the visitor wishes to do so, he can follow other possible routes.

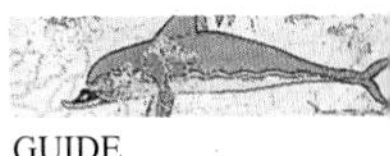



In the near future the visitors' route will undergo some alterations and some areas will be cordoned off. Generally speaking, however the route suggested here will be followed. After the tour of the palace and the houses around it in the main archaeological area, we recommend that visitors see another three large structures beyond this area: a tomb, and two monuments of Roman times, the Villa Dionysus and a mausoleum.

*Reconstitution of the Palace (According to C. Iliakis)*

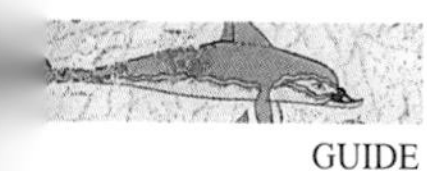



## A. THE PALACE

To get to the main archaeological site, one follows the Herakleion-Viannos road. Outside the palace there is a parking lot.

Beyond the entrance and the ticket booths, a refreshment bar and a stand where books and postcards are on sale, the palace tour begins.

### WEST WING

The visitor today enters the palace area by a modern stepped construction built on the site of the ancient west entrance, and immediately finds himself in the great paved WEST COURT of the palace (A), which is bounded on the western side by a retaining wall. At the further end, to the east, can be seen the partially restored western façade of the palace. Three

*'The West Court.*

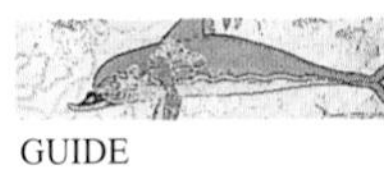

*The western façade of the Palace.*

processional ways (3) forming a triangle and raised slightly above the level of the ground, run across the court. In the southwestern corner stands the bust of Sir Arthur Evans, the archaeologist who excavated Knossos, a monument placed there in his honour by the Municipality of Herakleion.

The three large walled pits we see, known as "*kouloures*" (1), were intended to receive the refuse and the offerings from the ritual ceremonies which were held in the west court, as the two low altars (2) indicate. The west court had a formal and religious function and was linked by means of a processional way on its northern side to the "theatre". In the deeper strata under the court, the remains of the prepalatial and Neolithic settlements of the hill have been uncovered.

*Above left: The South Entrance.*
*Below left: The southwestern corner of the Palace.*
*Right: Reconstitution of the West Portico (according to C. Iliakis).*

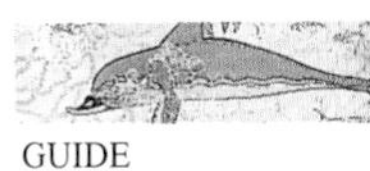



From the west court visitors enter the palace, passing through the monumental West Entrance (4), a columned portico (height of column = five metres), and the guard-room, and continue along the paved processional way (5), whose walls were adorned with the famous "frescoes of the Procession". The corridor has been restored with a wooden floor in its southern section which leads to the wide South

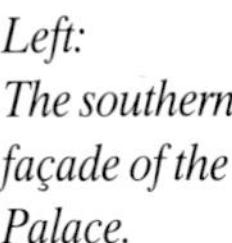

*Left:*
*The southern façade of the Palace.*

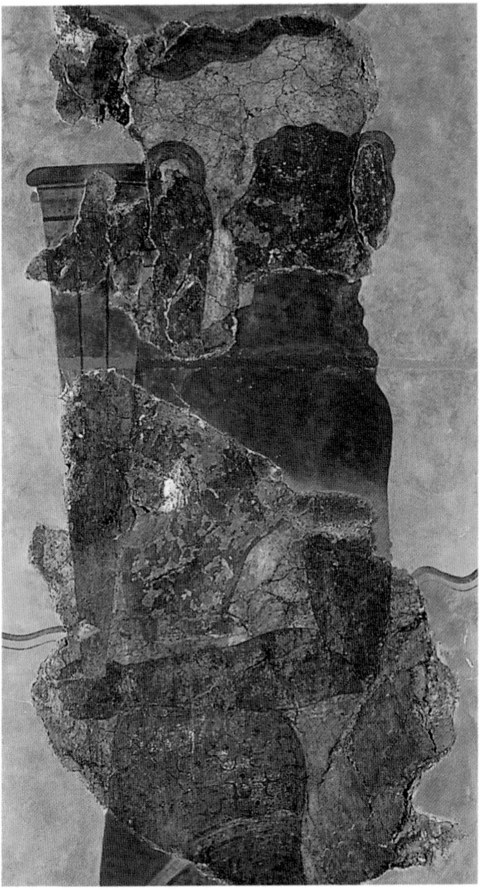

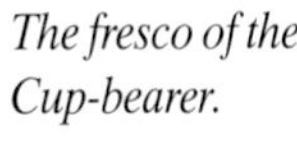

*The fresco of the Cup-bearer.*

Propylaeum. (6) where ended the stepped portico that led from the guest house over the viaduct, and which constituted the initial south entrance. After its destruction around 1600 BC, a new smaller south entrance was built, which led through an L- shaped corridor to the southwestern corner of the central court. The

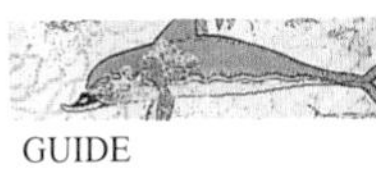
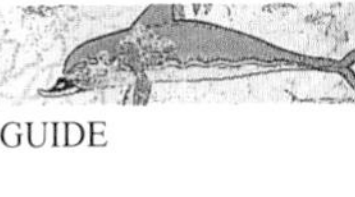



western section of the south propylaeum has been restored, and this is where a replica of part of the "fresco of the Procession" has been placed. The south propylaeum had two columns in the front and back of the wide portal, which closed from the south side. The pithoi we see there belong to the period when

*The South Propylaeum of the Palace.*

the palace site was reoccupied. From the south propylaeum the visitor ascends a wide staircase (7) to the restored first floor of the west wing (the *piano nobile*, according to Evans). The partly roofed, today, ground floor of the west wing includes the MAGAZINES (B), the THRONE ROOM system (C), and the CENTRAL SHRINE system (D).

To the east of the grand staircase is a rectangular structure (17) which Arthur Evans initially thought to be a "Mycenean palace" and later a "Greek" temple dedicated to the goddess Rhea, the latter theory being the more plausible.

On the first floor there were large colonnaded ceremonial rooms, which have been given conventional names (the "Shrine Room", the "Great Hall", etc.) (8). These rooms were adorned with beautiful frescoes, among which the famous fresco of the "Offerings", the "Parisienne", the miniature of the three-columned shrine, etc.

From the restored roof of the western wing one can see the eighteen large WEST MAGAZINES, which extend over the entire western half of the wing. The magazines are oblong rooms which have openings to the west towards the long and wide paved corridor (9). The large pithoi are lined up along two rows of deep square reservoirs whose sides are faced with gypsum slabs, and which served as storage containers for liquids, while the jars were used mainly to store dry supplies. There were jars and storage compartments in the corridor, too.

*The west wing.*

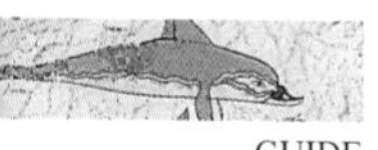



The magazines and the corridor provided space for a total of 400 jars, although only 150 were actually found there. They had an estimated total capacity of 80,000 litres. Various symbols were incised on the walls of the magazines: double axes, stars, branches, etc. which indicate the sacred nature of these rooms. Signs of the fire that destroyed the palace are still visible in various parts of the magazines.

In a covered room above the Throne Room are displayed a number of replicas of frescoes

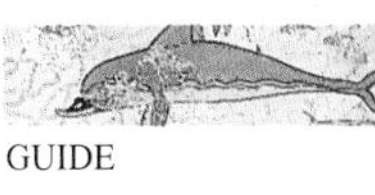

*The West Magazines.*

*The fresco of the "Parisienne".*

*Detail of a fresco representing a scene from the "taurokathapsia" (Archaeological Museum of Herakleion).*

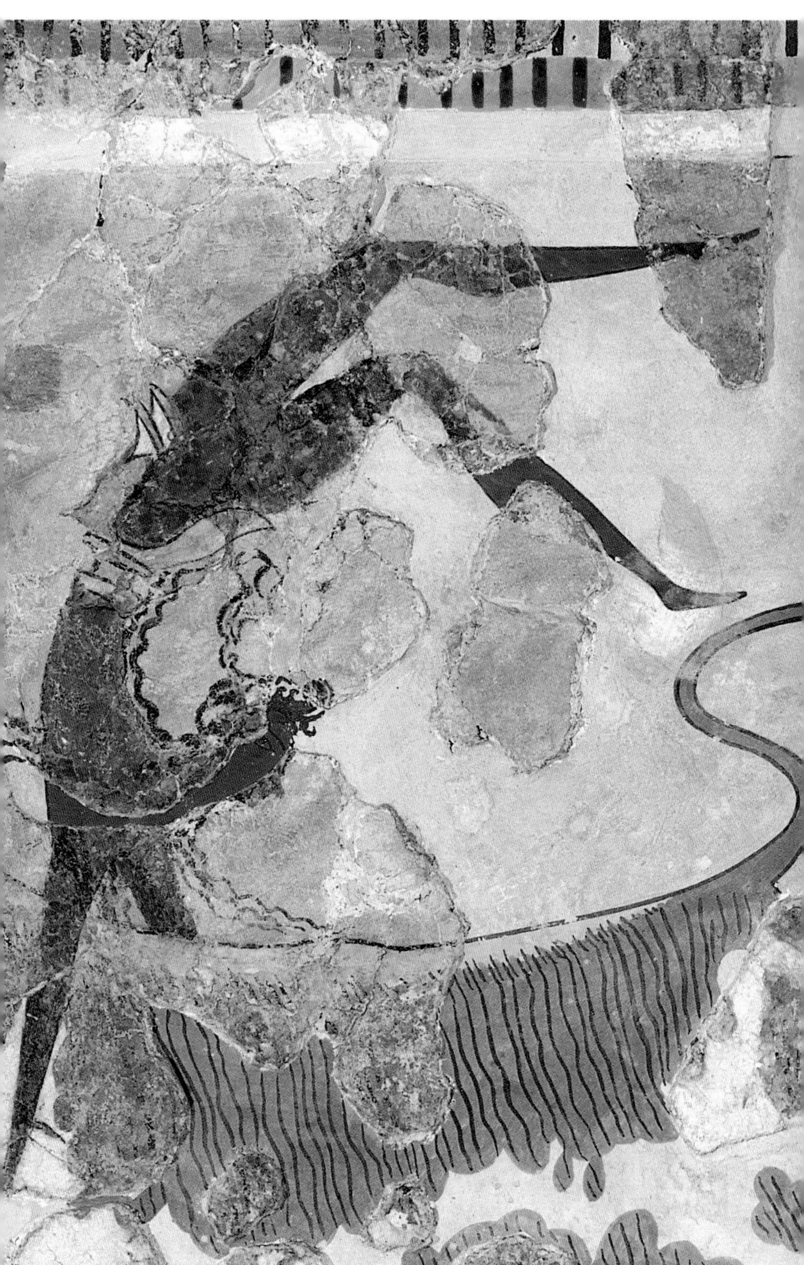

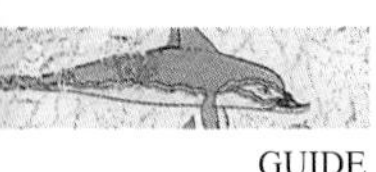

*Detail of the wall-painting of the "celebration before the shrine".*

which adorned various parts of the palace: the miniature frescoes of the “festivities before the shrine” and of the “dance in the sacred wood”, the frescoes of the “Ladies in Blue”, of the

"Toreador", of the "Nautilus", of the "Blue Monkey", of the "Blue Bird", and that of the "Captain of the Blacks".

From this room a small set of steps brings

*(Archaeological museum of Herakleion).*

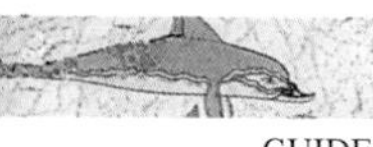



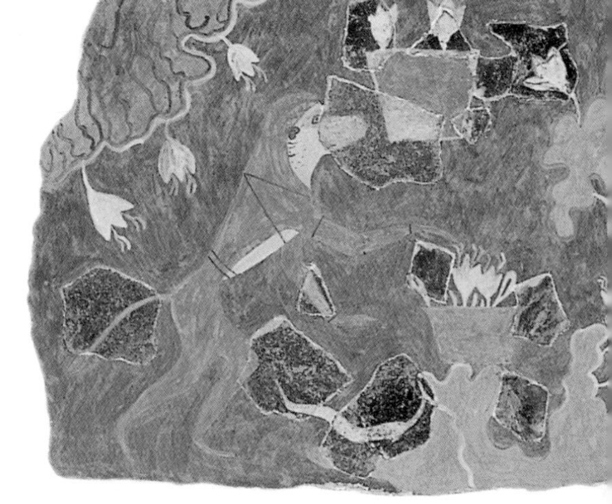

*The "Blue Monkey" fresco.*

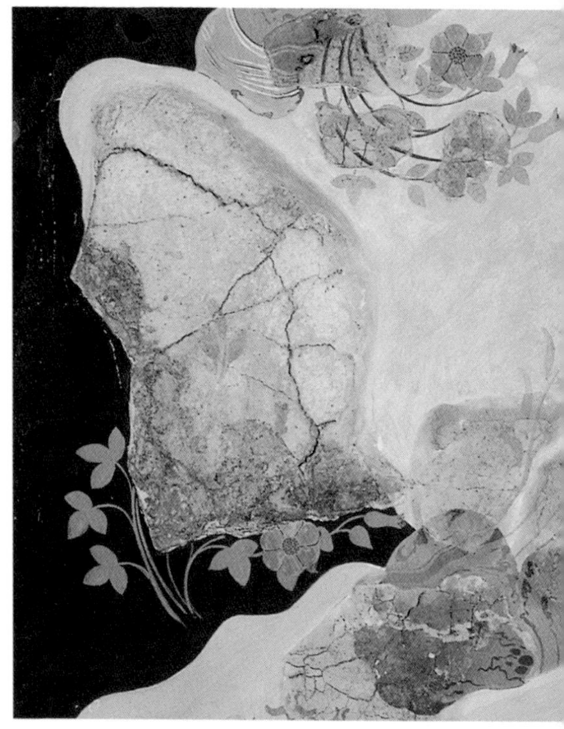

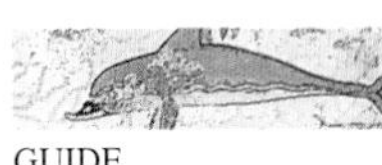



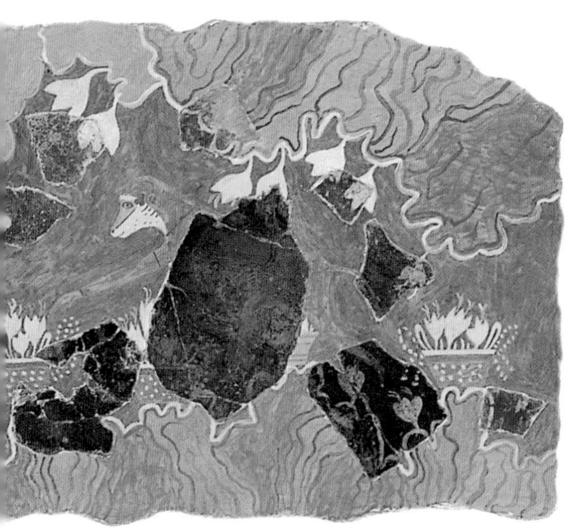

*The"Blue Bird" fresco.*

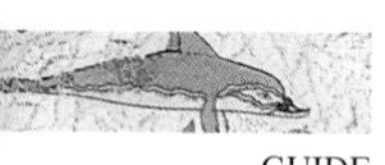

*Restored staircase leading to the second storey.*

one down to the antechamber of the throne room.

From the first floor of the west wing, the visitor descends by the grand double-colonnaded west stairway (10) to the large, paved rectangular CENTRAL COURT (E). Anyone wishing to pass from one wing of the palace to the other passed through this court, which served as a light-well and an air shaft for the palace which towered, many-storeyed, around it. It has been

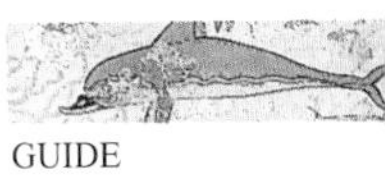



conjectured that various festivities and ceremonies took place in this central court. This is where the north and south entrance abutted. Its paved floor has only survived in the northwestern and southwestern corners.

Its pavement slabs, together with enormous quantities of other building stones of the palace were transported to Candia and used in the construction of its defensive wall during the period of Venetian rule. In the lower strata

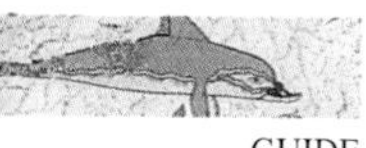



of the court, the successive phases of the Neolithic settlement were excavated and studied.

*The Throne Room System.*

From the central court, one can start to visit the THRONE ROOM system (C), which, in the form in which it has survived, dates, from the fourth phase of the new palace, the so-

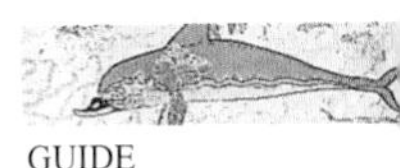



called "Mycenean" phase. Two steps down, and through the *polythyron*, a room with several pier-and-door partitions, the visitor comes first into the antechamber (11), which has a gypsum bench on the north and south sides, and a low platform on which, stood a wooden throne. In the middle of the antechamber

*The Throne Room.*

*The antechamber of the Throne Room.*

there is a basin made of porphyry. Here, during the excavations, were found the squat "*alabastra*" (perfume bottles or ointment vases) which were hastily abandoned when disaster struck the palace. Access to the main hall (12) is through a double entrance. Here we find the gypsum throne in the centre of the north wall, and benches on the north, west and south sides. There is also a "lustral area" (13) on the

*pp. 90-91: The "Throne of Minos". (Archaeological Museum of Herakleion).*

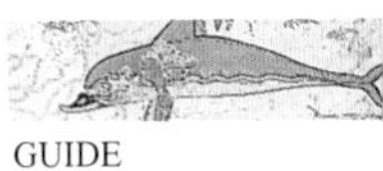



south side. To the right and left of the throne there are reproductions of the fresco with the griffins. These imaginary creatures, with the head of an eagle and body of a lion, symbolize royal and divine power.

This room had a religious function, and Evans believed that it was perhaps here that Minos met with the priesthood, who were also charged with the administration of justice. It is

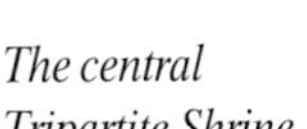

*The central Tripartite Shrine.*

*Faience figurines of the "Goddess of the Snakes" from the treasury of the central shrine of Knossos. Circa 1600 BC. (Herakleion Museum).*

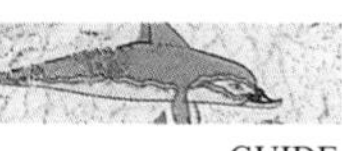



for this reason that a wooden replica of the throne was made in the Hague, for the president of the International Court of Justice. To the west and north of the room there are closed areas, with ledges built to hold the idols of the goddess and other cult objects and vessels.

South of the throne room complex we find the complex of the CENTRAL SHRINE (D), immediately south of the west staircase. Here is the Tripartite Shrine (14), whose façade is familiar to us from the fresco of the same name, and the Treasury of the Shrine (15) consisting of square, walled pits, where the famous snake goddesses and other ritual objects of the shrine were kept. To the west there are two rooms with a central square pillar. The square pillars are inscribed with sacred symbols and in front and behind them are small stone basins for liquid offerings. This, then, is where some kind of pillar worship took place, as the divinity was believed to inhabit them.

Crossing the central court to the south, we come to where the last portion of the Processional Way (18) has been restored. On the wall, has been placed a replica of the relief fresco known as the fresco of the "Priest King". He is portayed surrounded by lilies and leading a griffin or a sphinx by a rope which he holds in his hand.

Recently, it has been claimed that the pieces of the fresco represent three figures, two boxers and a priestess wearing a magnificent crown.

*The fresco of the "Prince with the Lilies" or of the "Priest-King" (Herakleion Museum).*

## East Wing

In the middle of the central court, we find the Grand Staircase (19), from where the visit of the east wing of the palace begins. This is where we shall find the ROYAL APARTMENTS (F), the HALL OF THE DOUBLE AXES (G), the EAST HALL (I), and the WORKSHOPS AREA (H). The ruins in this part of the palace were found in relatively good condition because the walls survived to

*The East Wing of the Palace.*

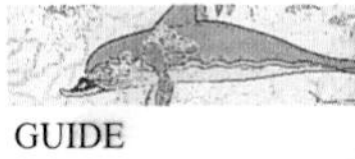

*The Grand Staircase.*

a fair height, thanks to the fact that the structure was built into a cutting of a slope, eight metres below the level of the central court. This allowed the palace to be built to a height of five storeys (the ground floor being level with the bottom of the cutting and supporting four floors above it) while, in the west wing, it was three storeys high (one at the level of the court and two above it). The ground floor and the upper floors of the “royal apartments” communicated by means of a monumental system of stairways, known as the Grand Staircase.

The Grand Staircase with the gypsum steps is one of the wonders of Minoan architecture. It consists of two wings of staircases, repeated

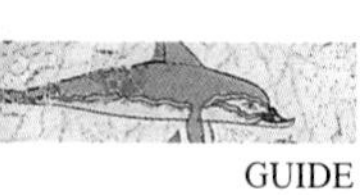



at each floor level. It is lit by a large light well situated to the east, and is surrounded by colonnades which create successive porches. Four flights have been preserved: the two upper ones have been restored, while the two lower ones are as they were found.

The great width of the staircase, the low tread and slight slant of the steps, facilitating ascent or descent, are worthy of notice. The

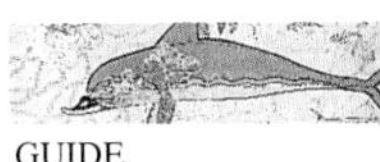



"Balcony of the Guards" owes its name to the great figure-of-eight shields which were painted on its walls (now shown in replica).

Having taken the stairs down to the ground level and followed the corridor to the east, the visitor comes to the "King's Megaron" also known as the "Hall of the Double Axes" (21), which has been given this name from this sacred symbol which has been incised on

*The "King's Megaron" viewed from the south.*

the blocks of the walls around. The Megaron consists of the main hall with the *polythyra* and porticoes to the west, east and south which look onto light wells. In the western portico were found the ruins of a stately throne which had been buried under a great block of porous limestone. The throne was a

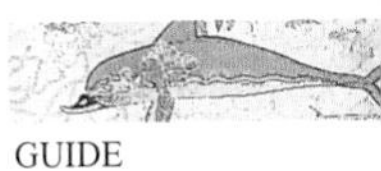
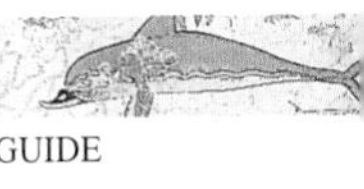



wooden one and was surrounded by small columns which held up a canopy. Today it is protected by a glass case. The polythyra were closed by double doors, which could be drawn inside the jambs, thus forming a single space where a large number of people could assemble, and, at the same time, creating a draught

*A section of the "Balcony with the Shields"*

*pp. 104-105: The "Queen's" Megaron.*

*Right: The "Queen's Bath"*

to cool the room. A wooden throne may perhaps have stood against the north wall. The walls of the Megaron, of the upper floor and of the verandah were adorned with frescoes of figure-of-eight shields, of a nautilus and of a bull, which have partially survived. They date from the third palatial "Mycenean period".

From the "King's Megaron" the visitor follows a corridor and reaches the "Queen's Megaron" (22), which is slightly smaller but sumptuously built, with multiple windows and benches, a portico and a light-well and with auxiliary areas: a bathroom with a clay tub, a toilet and a dressing room.

A small shrine on the floor above the megaron was a wonderful treasure trove which yielded a number of small objects: an ivory acrobat or "taurokathaptis" and other ivory pieces depicting various figures a bull, a tiny

*Ivory figurine of a "bull-leaper".*

18.

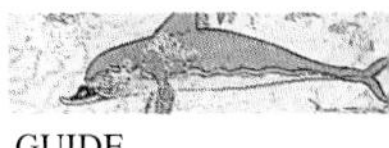



golden fish etc. Here, too, was found the gold and ivory “Boston goddess” which was unearthed before the excavations began, and smuggled out of the country. The “Queen’s Megaron” was adorned with marvellous frescoes (of dolphins, dancers, spirals, etc.).

Between the two megara and around them were stairways linking the various rooms and floors. A system of light-wells provided light and air.

The southern part of the east wing is occupied by the “Shrine of the Double Axes” (G), a complex which dates - in the form we see it today - from the “Mycenean phase” of the palace. Here there is a bench-altar (23), where the idols of the divinity and other cult objects were placed.

*Left above: The "fresco of the Dancing Girl". (Archaeological Museum of Herakleion).*

*Left below: the "Dolphin fresco". (Archaeological Museum of Herakleion).*

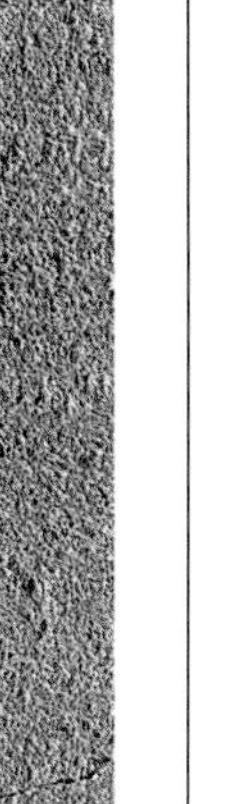

*Detail from the "Shrine of the Double Axes".*

*The workshop area.*

*Partial view of the lapidary's workshop.*

There is also a "lustral area", while pyramid-shaped stone bases for double axes were found here, as well.

From the Shrine of the Double Axes the visitor must return to the outside corridors of the megara and from there continue his tour in the area of the PALACE WORKSHOPS (8). Here stood the Lapidary's Workshop (25), and the lumps of Spartan basalt on which he was working can still be seen as he left them when disaster struck.

Next to it is the Potter's Workshop (26), with a low bench and a plaster basin for

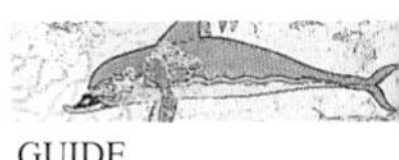



moulding the clay. A room above the potter's workshop was adorned with the fresco of the "Taurokathapsia" ("Toreador" fresco). North of the workshop is the "Court of the Stone Spout" (27). To the east is the stepped East Entrance (29), with a system for the drainage of rainwater consisting of conduits running down the sides of the steps and of drainage wells at intervals.

North of the narrow modern stairway are the Magazines of the Giant Pithoi (28), which belong to the period of the old palace. Further north were the potters' workshops and the Northeast Magazines (34) of the old palace.

Taking the small modern stairway to the west, the visitor ascends to the space once occupied by the GREAT EAST HALL (I), the

*Pithoi decorated with relief medallions from the Magazines of the Pithoi.*

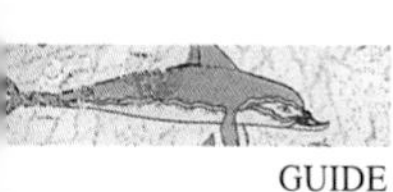

*Above:*
*The fresco of the "Ladies in Blue". (Herakleion Museum).*

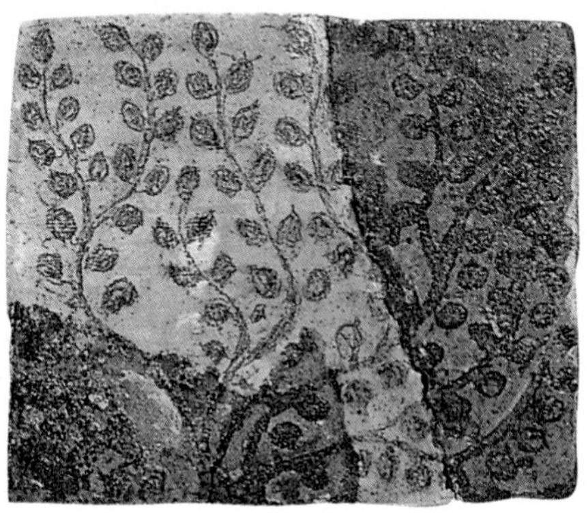

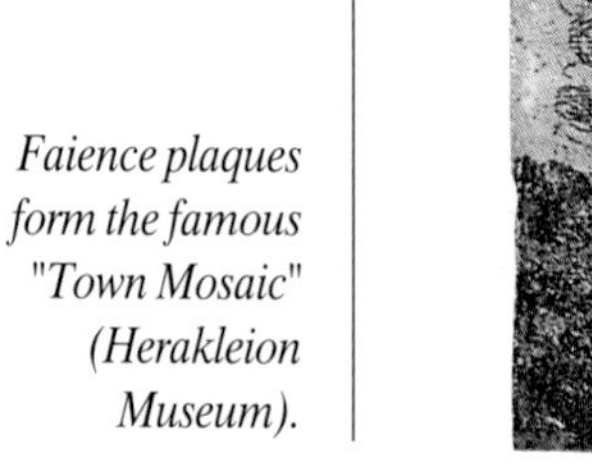

*Faience plaques form the famous "Town Mosaic" (Herakleion Museum).*

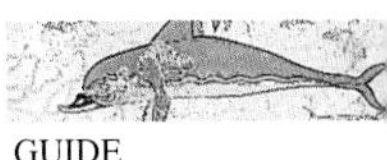



ground floor of which has now been restored and covered. Here is the Magazine of the Medallion Pithoi (30).

The fresco of the "Ladies in Blue" was found in this area. In one of the small rooms was also found the famous "Town Mosaic", consisting of faience plaques representing the façades of Minoan houses.

All these finds come from the storey occupied by the Great Hall. Here, too, we find the Corridor of the Bays (32).

The Great East Hall is thought to have been the formal throne room. In this hall stood the colossal *xoanon* (wooden cult stat-

*The "Corridor of the Bays"'.*

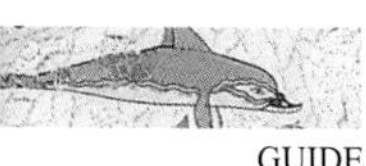



ue) of the Great Goddess, of which only the bronze plaits of hair have been preserved, while charred masses of wood were found during the excavations on the northern side of the hall. The height of the statue is estimated to have been 2.80 m. The walls of the hall were adorned with the magnificent reliefs depicting scenes of athletic contests and griffins tied to a column.

North of the Great Hall are various areas, such as the "Corridor of the Draughtboard" (33), where the famous royal gaming table re-

*The northeastern sector of the Palace.*

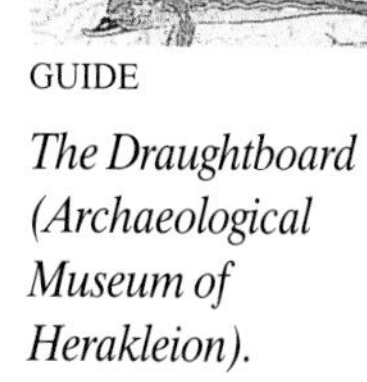



*The Draughtboard (Archaeological Museum of Herakleion).*

sembling a chessboard was found. Sections of the drainage system have been preserved and can be seen here. Other areas have also been given conventional names: the Northeast Hall, the East Magazines, the Olive Press etc. The area with the partitions perhaps served as

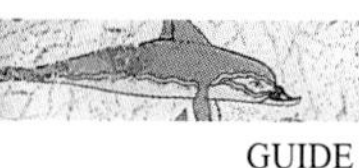



*pp. 116-117: The northern sector.*

*The relief "fresco of the Bull".*

*The North Entrance to the Palace. View of one of the porches.*

kennels or stables for the palace animals. Passing along the northeast magazines, the visitor finds himself in the complex of the NORTH ENTRANCE (J), where there is the large northern pillared hall, known as the "Customs House" (36). This large hall had three aisles with eight square pillars supporting the roof. This is where the harbour road ended, and archaeologists have conjectured that this is where the goods unloaded from the ships were brought. It is also possible that it may have served as a banquet hall. From the Customs House begins the ramp of the North Entrance (37) leading to the "Central Court". On either side of the ramp were imposing balconies. One of the balconies ("bastion") has been restored; on it has been set a replica of the relief fresco of the Charging Bull.

*pp. 120-121: View of the North Entrance to the Palace.*

*Above: The "North Lustral Area".*

The last sector of the palace which must be visited is the NORTHWEST SECTOR (K) - or "*Northwest Insula*" according to Evans. Here there are six very deep basement rooms (39), which are enclosed by a rectangular wall. Evans called these rooms "cells", but they could have been storerooms. They belong to the old palace. Above the "cells", during the period of the new palace, a shrine with a paved floor and a square pillar in the centre was built. The upper part was adorned with frescoes. Here were found the fragments of the miniature frescoes of the Tripartite Shrine, of the Sacred Wood and of the

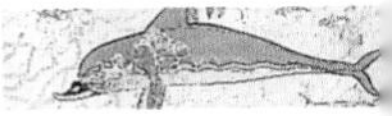

*The Royal Way.*

Saffron Gatherer. One of the rooms of this area contained a large number of tablets with inscriptions in Linear B script. North of this area is the restored North "Lustral Area" (38).

As he leaves the palace, on the western side, the visitor comes to the famous and unique THEATRAL AREA (L) of Knossos. This was one of the ceremonial areas of the palace and of the city of Knossos. The seats have been arranged in two intersecting "wings" (40), the east and the south wing. At the point where the two wings meet, was the "Royal Box". The theatre is thought to have

been able to accommodate 400 spectators. This is where the famous paved ROYAL ROAD with the processional corridor ended.

It led to the Little Palace after passing through the city. Some of the larger and more

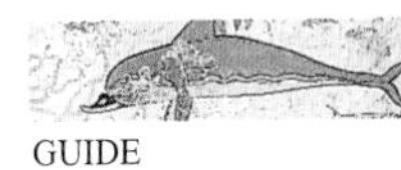



important houses of the city stood along the Royal Road (The House of the Frescoes, etc.)

From the Theatral Area, the visitor returns to the West Court, and from there to the exit of the archaeological site.

*The Theatral Area.*

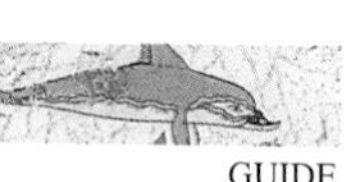



# THE HOUSES AROUND THE PALACE

Some of the most interesting excavated houses of the city are to be found within the fenced-in main archaeological site and can be visited. In relation to the palace, the "House of the Frescoes" is to the northwest, the "South House", as its name indicates, to the

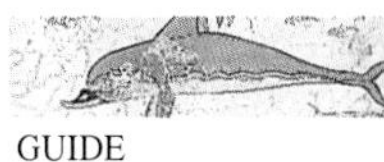
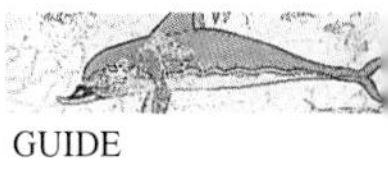



south, while the "House of the Fallen Blocks", the "House of the Sacrificed Oxen", the "House of the High Priest" (or of the Chancel Screen) and the "Southeast House" lie to the southeast. The "House of the Frescoes" is situated south of the Royal Road and owes its name to the stack of fragmented frescoes found in one of its rooms. These frescoes are among the most famous of Knossos: they in-

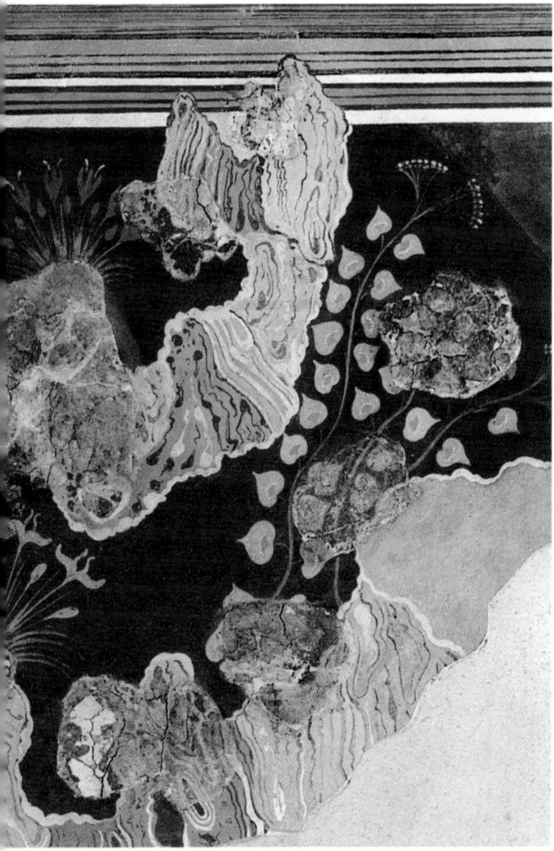

*Detail from the fresco of the "Blue Monkey" (Archaeological Museum of Herakleion).*

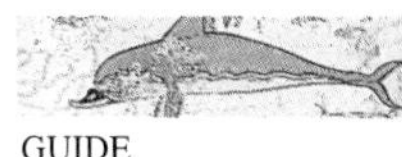



clude the “Blue Bird”, the “Blue Monkey”, the “Gardens” and the “Captain of the Blacks”. Replicas of these frescoes are now in the room above the Throne Room in the palace.

The “South House” is situated at a lower level than the Palace, below its southwestern corner. It was built beside the stepped portico during the second neopalatial period, when that portico fell into disuse. It was a three-storey structure and was restored by Sir Arthur Evans. Recently, new work has begun to strengthen the structure. It has some very interesting architectural features: a pillar crypt, a “Lustral Area”, a stand for a double axe, etc. Among the finds in this house, worth mentioning is the discovery of a hoard of silver vessels and a set of bronze tools.

The “House of the Sacrificed Oxen” and the “House of the Fallen Blocks” date from the first neopalatial period. Their names are due to the discovery, in the former, of remains of a sacrifice (a tripod altar and horns of a bull) and, in the latter, to the blocks of stone which were hurled into the house from the façade of the palace during the earthquake. The “House of the Chancel Screen” has a dais and a partition with two columns. The “Southeast House” was adorned with frescoes of lilies. It has a *polythyron,* a pillar crypt and a stand for a double axe. Here, a beautiful lamp of porphyry was also found. The remainder of the houses and monuments are situated outside the enclosed area of the Palace.

*The fresco of the “Seated Priestess‘”. (Archaeological Museum of Herakleion).*

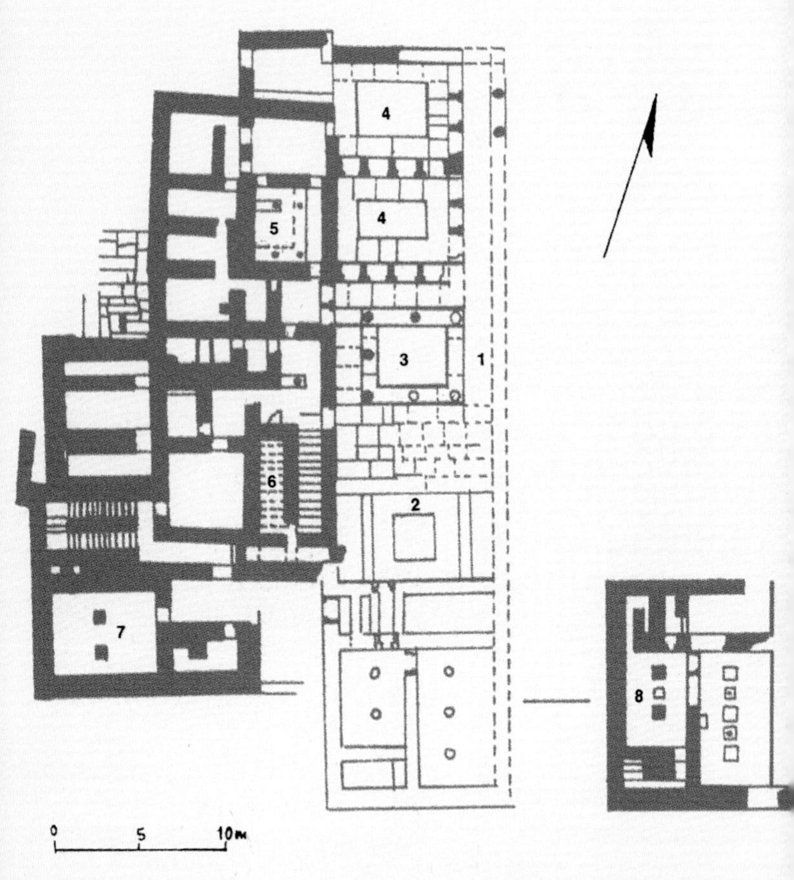

4
4
5
3
1
6
2
7
8
0
5
10m

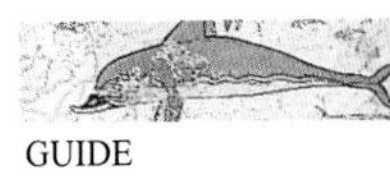



# THE "LITTLE PALACE" AND THE "UNEXPLORED MANSION"

These are to the west of the tarred road, before the entrance to the modern settlement. The Little Palace covers approximately 1500 sq. metres and is lavishly built, with all the architectural features which are to be found in the Great Palace.

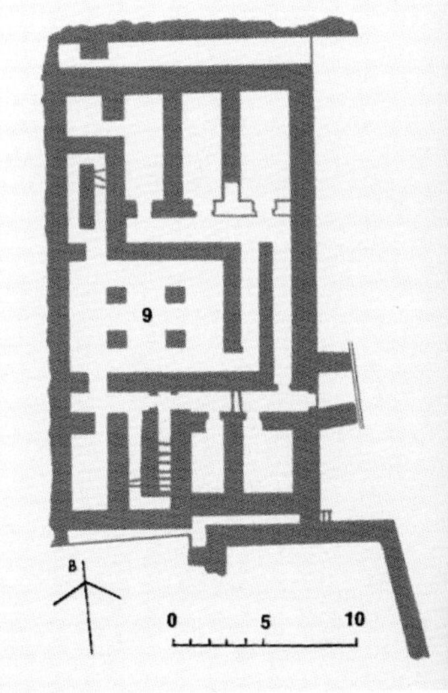


Its Entrance (1), to the east, led to stately reception areas: the Entrance Hall (2), the Hall of the Peristyle (3), a double Megaron with *polythyra* (4) and a portico to the east. It also had a "lustral area", which was transformed, during the postpalatial period, into a "Fetish shrine" (5).

*Ground plan of the "Unexplored mansion"*

A Grand Staircase led to the upper floor. There were also pillar crypts on the ground floor beneath the entrance (8) and in the southwestern corner (7). In a repository near the southwestern crypt was found the magnificent steatite rhyton in the shape of a bull's head, now in the Herakleion Museum.

A paved way and a small flagstoned court to the west separates the "Little Palace" from the "Unexplored Mansion" (9), which was excavated about twenty years ago, and of which only the impressive western façade was known. This mansion was linked to the Little

*Ground plan of the "Little Palace".*

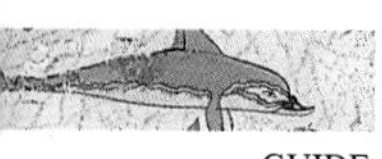



Palace by a bridge. It was built during the second neopalatial period and was used again during the "Mycenean phase" and therafter. It is rectangular in shape and was built with skilfully hewn blocks of stone. It has a central hall with four square pillars, corridors, magazines and a stairway to the upper floor.

## THE "ROYAL VILLA", THE "GUEST HOUSE" AND THE "SACRED SPRING"

The Royal Villa is situated to the northeast of the palace, south of the settlement of Makrys Toichos. It is built into a cutting in the side of the hill and overlooks the Kairatos valley. Its construction is luxurious and has been carried out with meticulous care. The entrance is through an anteroom (1), into the Megaron with its row of three doors (polythyra) (2), where there is a semicircular recess on the west side for the throne (3) and columns on a partition.

*Ground plan of the Royal Villa*

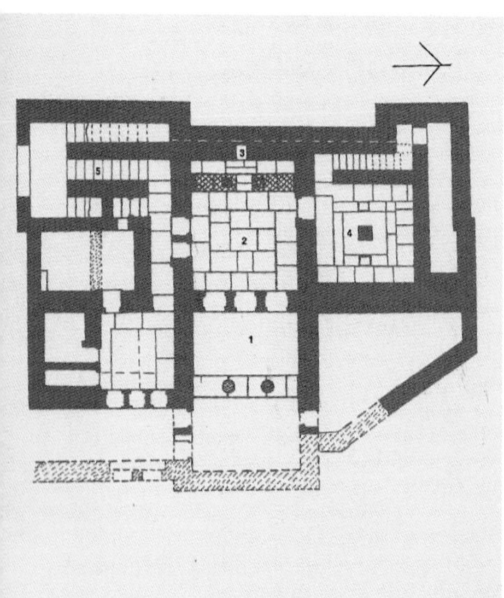


It also has a pillar crypt with a single square pillar (4) and in the floor there are

*Detail from the "Partridge" fresco. (Archaeological Museum of Herakleion).*

small stone basins to catch the liquid offerings. A double stairway (5) led to the upper floor, where the entrance to the Villa was perhaps situated.

The Guest House is situated to the south, opposite the Palace, to which it is linked by the viaduct. It was thought to have been used for receiving guests coming to Knossos from the south. In a room which has been restored today was found the famous fresco with the partridges. (A replica has been set in its place). The other room was a bathroom.

West of the Guest House (or Caravanserai) complex was the Spring Chamber, where the water of the Vlychiá spring welled up until only recently. The room has ledges for offerings and a niche for a lamp. We have here an interesting example of a "spring shrine".

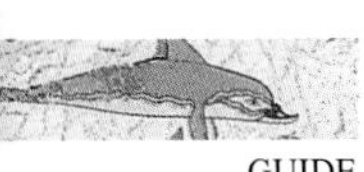



## THE SOUTH ROYAL TEMPLE TOMB

This is the southernmost monument of Minoan Knossos and is situated at a distance of approximately 600 metres from the palace. Its construction is perfect, with dressed blocks of poros stone - a royal edifice indeed. It combines the function of tomb and shrine and is a unique monument of prehistoric Greece. It was excavated following the chance discovery here of a golden ring, the famous ring of Minos, which has since been lost.

The temple tomb consists of an entrance, through a court with a portico, a small antechamber, a pillar crypt with two square pillars and a rock-cut burial chamber with walls lined with gypsum slabs and a square gypsum pier in the middle. The finds date one of the last burials in the main burial chamber to the

*Ground plan and elevation of the "South Royal Temple Tomb".*

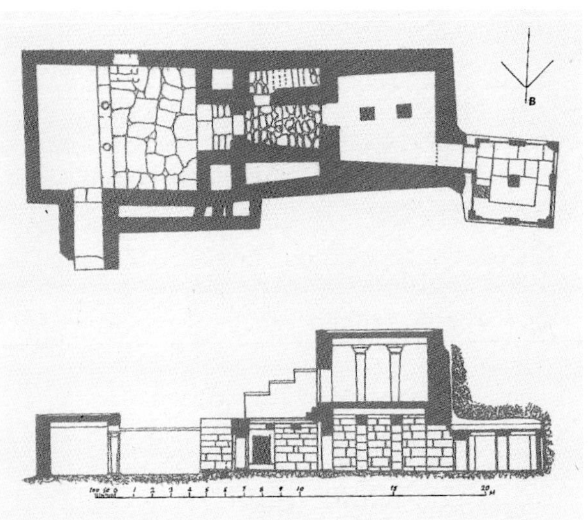

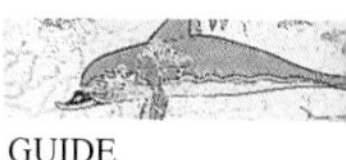

*Gold ring from the tomb at Isopata. (Archaeological Museum of Herakleion).*

Mycenean phase of Knossos. Sir Arthur Evans believed that this is where the last Minos was buried. A stairway leads to the upper floor, which had two columns. The edifice was crowned with the double horns of consecration.

This tomb greatly resembles the tomb described by Diodorus as having been built for Minos in Sicily and which consisted of a tomb below and a shrine above.

To the west and north of the royal tomb, at Gypsades, are the so-called "Hogarth's Houses" . These were large and important mansions which were named after the British archaeologist who excavated them in the early years of this century.

Another royal tomb in Knossos and also quite unique, was the famous TOMB OF ISOPATA, situated at a distance of 2,5 kilometres to the north of the palace.

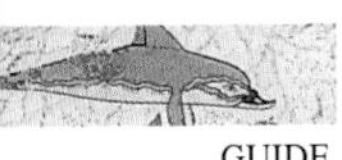



This tomb had a rock-cut dromos, a built vestibule and an oblong burial chamber roofed by a stone vault.

Unfortunately this unique monument was ruthlesly torn down by the Germans during the war and its material used for the construction of a pill-box.

*Marble statue of the emperor Hadrian. (Archaeological Museum of Herakleion).*

## THE VILLA DIONYSUS

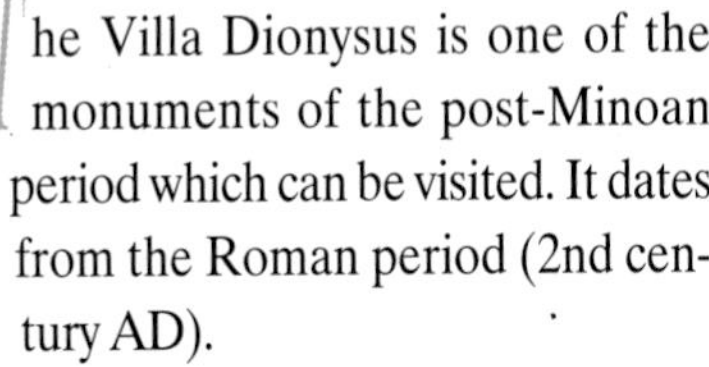

The Villa Dionysus is one of the monuments of the post-Minoan period which can be visited. It dates from the Roman period (2nd century AD).

The villa is situated in the enclosed area of the Villa Ariadne, 250 metres to the north. It owes its name to its unique mosaic floors which portray the god Dionysus.

In the centre, of the villa is a peristyle with Doric columns of poros stone. To the west is the "*oikos*", and to the north and south other rooms, all of them with mosaic floors decorated with Dionysiac scenes and geometric patterns. Here was found the statue of the emperor Hadrian which is now in the Archaeological Museum of Herakleion.

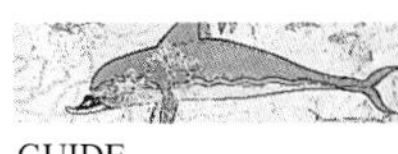



## THE MAUSOLEA ON THE UNIVERSITY GROUNDS

A group of mausolea which have been preserved in the area north of the University, and between the University and the Venizeleion Hospital date from the same period. These monumental tombs are built underground or above ground and are constructed of dressed poros stone. They usually have a descending stairway, a low entrance with monolithic jambs and lintel, and a rectangular chamber with monolithic funerary beds standing on stone legs. The roof, of hewn stone may be flat or cylindrical.
The finds date the tombs to the period between the 2nd and the 4th century AD. Some were destroyed by the earthquake of 365 AD.

*Marble statue of Dionysus. (Archaeological Museum of Herakleion).*

# EPILOGUE

*Here ends our visit to Knossos. We hope the visitor to the ruins of this unique Minoan palace and city has formed a vivid picture of the splendid first Hellenic civilization. However, this picture would not be complete without a visit to the Archaeological Museum of Herakleion, where the treasures from the excavations at Knossos are displayed.*

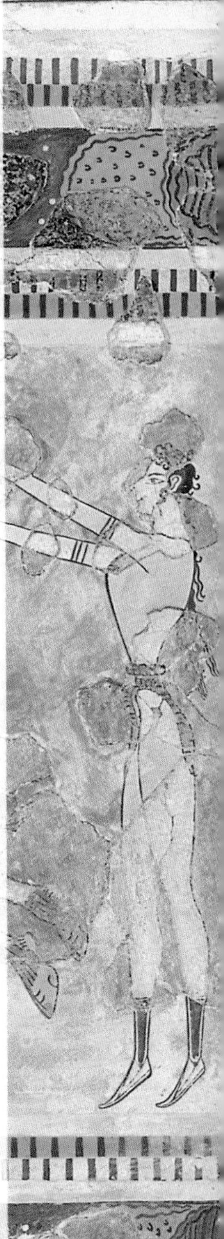

# SELECT BIBLIOGRAPHY

ALEXIOU, ST., *Μινωϊκός πολιτισμός, με οδηγό των ανακτόρων: Ανάκτορον Κνωσού*, 131-196 (Herakleion 1964)

BROCK J., *Fortetsa: Early Greek Tombs near Knossos* (Cambridge 1957)

BROWN A. *Arthur Evans and the Palace of Minos* (Oxford 1983)

CADOGAN G., *The Palaces of Minoan Crete: Knossos 50-91*, (London and New York 1976

CADOGAN G., MYERS E. and J. *The Aerial Atlas of Ancient Crete*

CHADWICK J., O Μινωϊκός Κόσμος (Athens 1996) (Berkeley 1992), 127-147

COLDSTREAM J.N., *Knossos: The Sanctuary of Demeter* (London 1973)

COLDSTREAM J.N., *et al., Knossos: The North Cemetery (*London *1996)*

EVANS A.J.*: The Palace of Minos at Knossos*, vols. I-IV (London 1921-1935)

EVANS J., *et al. Excavations in the Neolithic Settlement at Knossos*, I, II (London 1964-1968)

EVANS J., Neolithic Knossos: The Growth of a Settlement, *Proceedings of the Prehistoric Society* (1971), 92-117.

GRAHAM W.J., *The Palaces of Crete: Knossos*, 23-33, 51-58 and passim (Princeton 1972)

HOOD M.S., *The Minoans*, 65-72 and passim (London 1971)

HOOD M.S., *The Bronze Age Palace at Knossos (Plan and Sections)* (London 1981)

HOOD M.S., *Archaeological Survey of the Knossos Area* (London 1981)

HUTCHINSON, R., *Prehistoric Crete, Knossos*: 170-

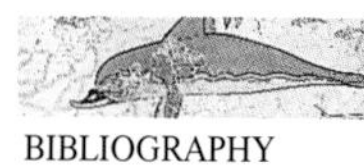



81, 270-9 and passim (Harmondsworth 1962)

KALOKAIRINOS M., Ανασκαφές στην Κνωσό, *Παλίμψηστον* 9/10, supplement, 5-69 (ed. K. Kopakas Herakleion 1990).

Knossos: *A Labyrinth of History* (Papers in Honour of Sinclair Hood, Oxford 1994).

KRONTIRA L. - VASSILAKIS A., *Πρώτη Γνωριμία με τη Κρήτη του Μίνωα* (Athens 1988)

MICHAILIDOU A., *Knossos, A Complete Guide to the Palace of Minos*

PENDLEBURY J., *A Handbook to the Palace of Knossos* (London 1954) and Greek translation by N. PLATON: *Οδηγός Κνωσσού* (Herakleion 1950)

PENDLEBURY J., *The Archaeology of Crete, Knossos*: (London 1939)

PLATON N., *Ιστορία του Ελληνικού Έθνους* A:, "Κνωσός" 170-9 (Athens 1970)

POPHAM M., *Minoan Unexplored Mansion* (London 1984)

POWELL D., *The Villa Ariadne* (London 1973)

SACKETT L.H. et al, *Knossos. From Greek City to Roman Colony: Excavations at the Unexplored Mansion II* (London 1992)

SAKELLARAKIS G. and E., *Κρήτη: Ιστορία και Πολιτισμός: Νεολιθική και Μινωϊκή Κρήτη*, 3-130 (Herakleion 1987)

SANDERS I., *Roman Crete*. 51-53, 67-70, 105-7, 152-3 (Wilts. 1982)

VASSILAKIS A., *Μινωϊκή Κρήτη με οδηγό των αρχαιολογικών χώρων: Κνωσός*, 178-190 (Herakleion 1992)

VASSILAKIS A., *Κρήτη* (Athens 1997)

VENTRIS M. - CHADWICK J., *Documents in Mycenean Greek* (Cambridge 1956)

ZOIS A., *Κρήτη, Εποχή του Λίθου: Κνωσός 133-174* (Athens 1973)

ZOIS A., *Κνωσός, Το Εκστατικό Όραμα* (Herakleion 1966).

# INDEX

## PLACE-NAMES



## INDEX OF PROPER NAMES

### ANCIENT

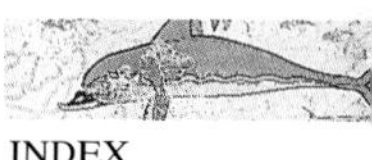





## MODERN



Abbreviations:
EMI: Early Minoan I
MMI: Middle Minoan I
LMI: Late Minoan I
Dating of periods according to Evans

ART EDITOR: Costas Adam
TEXT: Antonis Vassilakis
TEXT EDITOR: Kiki Birtacha
LAYOUT: Elena Christopoulou
PHOTOGRAPHS: Costas Adam, Yiannis Yiannelos,
Archaeological Receipts Fund
ENGLISH TRANSLATION: Daphne Kapsambelis
PRODUCED BY: PERGAMOS S.A.